SUPPLEMENT TO THE LYON IN MOURNING

PRINCE CHARLES EDWARD STUART

ITINERARY AND MAP

THE CAVE IN GLENMORISTON

VIEW OF INTERIOR, LOOKING OUTWARD

From a Sketch by Alex. Ross, Esq., LL.D.

ITINERARY

OF PRINCE

CHARLES EDWARD STUART

FROM HIS LANDING IN SCOTLAND JULY 1745

TO HIS DEPARTURE IN SEPTEMBER 1746

Compiled from THE LYON IN MOURNING
supplemented and corrected from other
contemporary sources by

WALTER BIGGAR BLAIKIE

With a Map

EDINBURGH

SCOTTISH ACADEMIC PRESS

1975

Published for the Scottish History Society

by

SCOTTISH ACADEMIC PRESS LTD.
25 Perth Street, Edinburgh
EH3 5DW

First published .   . 1897
Reprinted 1975

© The Scottish History Society 1975

ISBN 0 7073 0103 3

Printed in Great Britain by
T. & A. Constable Ltd., Edinburgh

CONTENTS

ILLUSTRATIONS

PREFACE

THE Itinerary now issued as a Supplement to *The Lyon in Mourning* originated in an attempt to compile a simple diary of the movements of Prince Charles Edward as they are recorded in the collections of Bishop Forbes. It was indeed intended to be no more than a chronological index which should form part of the third volume of that work. An analysis of the contents of *The Lyon*, however, soon revealed the existence of gaps in the narratives which needed to be filled up, and discrepancies, real or apparent, which required correction or explanation. This necessitated an examination and comparison of all the original sources available, and, in consequence, a considerable enlargement of the scope of the Itinerary, with the view of obtaining a complete daily record of the Expedition. The material thus collected has so far exceeded in bulk the work originally contemplated that the Council of the Scottish History Society has thought it convenient to issue this Supplement as a separate volume.

The Itinerary is not intended to be a history; but while the daily record is necessarily brief, the statements in the text have been so far expanded as to render them intelligible to the reader without the need of constant recurrence to their sources except for verification and amplification. For this reason the motives that inspired the various actions of the Prince have been set down wherever there has been found sufficient contemporary authority for doing so; and to make these motives for action clearer, brief statements of the movements of the opposing government troops have been interpolated in italic type.

An attempt has also been made to show of what forces the

Jacobite army was composed. Any such account, which must be largely compiled from the newspaper reports of the day, cannot pretend to absolute accuracy. It can, however, indicate generally, or with a certain approach to completeness, when and where and in what numbers the various bodies of his adherents joined Prince Charles Edward.

In an Additional Note, an endeavour has been made to form an estimate of the troops employed on both sides at critical periods of the campaign, and of the numbers engaged in the several battles.

Some original documents showing the tension between the Prince and his principal lieutenant, which had much influence on the conduct of the Expedition, are printed in an appendix.

While the Itinerary is not a history of the Adventure of 1745, care has been taken to make it approximately an index of authorities for such a history, and no statement of importance is made without reference to the original source from which it is derived. There has indeed been occasional difficulty in reconciling the various contemporary narratives, more especially during the Prince's wanderings after Culloden. Frequently statements are made, partly from what the narrator has picked up and partly from personal knowledge, but so blended as to make it difficult to distinguish the one from the other. In this part of the Itinerary care has been taken to follow as far as possible the statements of those only who at the time were present with the Prince, and to differentiate mere hearsay from actual knowledge.[1]

There are discrepancies even among the stories of eye-

---

[1] Home informs us that the Prince, 'from the beginning to the end of his wanderings, never told the people whom he left whither he was going, nor those to whom he came whence he had come' (H.H. 250 *n.*), and his friends, with characteristic Highland courtesy, seem not to have asked him. A conspicuous instance of this ignorance is to be found in the memorial of Lochgarry, who joined the Prince at Achnasual immediately after his return from Chisholm's country (*Itinerary*, p. 65). Lochgarry is ignorant of that visit, and erroneously narrates that the Prince had spent nearly a month in the cave in Glenmoriston (*Ibid.* P.S. p. 123).

witnesses, particularly in the matter of dates. This is little to be wondered at. Great accuracy was not to be expected in the circumstances, and it may also be assumed that the narratives were written from memory, often a considerable time after the events. When on analysis it has been found necessary to alter the dates given by the narrator, the reasons for making the change have been given fully in footnotes.

Where a statement is made from negative evidence only, it is prefaced by the word [probably].

Where no authority is indicated in the notes, the statements therein are derived from local investigations made either personally or by correspondence, and such notes, as a rule, embody the result of inquiries for Jacobite traditions in the places visited by Prince Charles Edward during the Expedition.

I have throughout avoided quoting authorities not strictly contemporary or original, with the exception of an occasional reference to Home's *History of the Rebellion*; and that work is in a sense contemporary, as it is written by a man who fought in the struggle; but Home is only quoted as collateral evidence, or when other sources of information fail. Considerable use, however, is made of his appendices of original documents.

A list of the authorities referred to in the Itinerary will be found at the end of this preface. Since the publications of Browne, Chambers, Jesse, and Ewald, the principal fresh materials of importance that have been printed are to be found in Colonel Allardyce's *Historical Papers of the Jacobite Period*, and in the Family Histories written by Sir William Fraser. Of these, which have been freely made use of, the most important is the Narrative of Lord MacLeod, son of the Earl of Cromarty, which, though occasionally misleading in detail through mistakes in dates, throws a good deal of light on the history of the Expedition.

I have had the privilege of access to several manuscript sources. The Duke of Atholl, the direct descendant of Lord George Murray, has kindly given me assistance and information from family papers and journals in his possession. Such information is indicated in the Itinerary by the initial (A). Miss Murray MacGregor has allowed me to peruse a most interesting narrative of the Clan MacGregor's movements in the '45, written by Duncan MacPharic or MacGregor, one of the Glengyles. Mr. John MacGregor, W.S., has permitted me to quote from a manuscript History of the MacGregor Clan now in his custody; Mr. Fitzroy Bell has placed at my disposal the original material he has collected for the elucidation of the papers and journals of John Murray of Broughton, which he is at present editing for the Scottish History Society; and a good deal of information has been obtained from manuscript State Papers.

I have not had the advantage of seeing the well-known manuscript Narrative of Lord Elcho, though occasionally in these pages passages from it are referred to which have been printed by other authors.

After this Itinerary was printed, a manuscript memorial written by MacDonell of Lochgarry was placed at my disposal by the kindness of Mr. Charles Fraser-Mackintosh; and with the permission of its proprietor, Mr. Æneas Ronald MacDonell, formerly of Morar, a near relative of Glengarry, and the representative of the historic family of Scotus, it is printed as a postscript to this volume.

This narrative gives information recorded nowhere else, and its recovery has made it possible to complete, with a near approach to certainty, the mapping of the routes taken by the Prince in his wanderings.

The Map of Scotland which accompanies this volume is on the scale of ten miles to the inch. It was at first intended to reproduce the contemporary map of Dorret, originally published in 1750, and on it to mark the various routes. On examination, however, the details of that map were found to be so faulty and imperfect, both geographically and topographically, that the plan of reproducing a truly contemporary map had to be abandoned, and it was thought best to use a modern map

founded on the Ordnance Survey. From this modern map the
railways and a large number of unnecessary names have been
removed for the sake of clearness.

Since the year 1745 many names have disappeared from the
map: townships and villages have been swept away; mansion
houses that conferred territorial dignity on their proprietors
or tenants have either ceased to exist or have become too
insignificant to find a place on a map of this scale. Nearly
all the important places mentioned in *The Lyon in Mourning*
have been restored, particular care being taken to include
the territorial names by which the Highland combatants are
generally referred to. In this way a large number of names—
many now obsolete—have been added to the map, and I have
to thank Mr. Bartholomew for the assistance he has given
me and the pains he has taken in identifying many obscure
pláces.

The modern roads have been retained here, because although
in 1745 few regular roads except those of Marshal Wade existed
in the Highlands, and not very many in the Lowlands, the nature
of the country makes it certain that the roads of modern times
are not far different from the tracks or routes then in use.

In some places the scale of this map is too small to allow
the reader to follow with accuracy the details of the Prince's
recorded movements; but in these cases references in the text
are so made that the movements may be easily traced on the
large-scale Ordnance maps.

No attempt has been made either on the map or in the text
to spell names of places correctly, or even consistently, or to
solve the vexed question of the spelling of Highland place-names.
It has been thought sufficient to make them recognisable.
Generally, the names are printed as they are found in Bishop
Forbes's manuscripts, where, as a rule, they are rude phonetic
renderings of the Gaelic; when they differ in spelling from the
Ordnance Survey so materially as to be recognised with difficulty,
the Ordnance spellings have been added within brackets.

The Clan divisions are based on the well-known Clan map of General Stewart of Garth. The constant changing of clan territory makes these divisions at best merely an approximation, and in one or two cases Garth's map is slightly modified to bring it into harmony with statements in *The Lyon*. For instance, North Morar, shown by Garth as Clanranald's, is here given to Glengarry (I. 332), and the boundary of the Chisholm's country is slightly altered to include part of Glenstrathfarrar in Fraser territory (III. 106).

I desire to express my grateful obligations for help from many sources in making this Itinerary. The Society is indebted to Her Majesty the Queen for permission to print a letter from the Prince to his father. Without the assistance of the present Lochiel (Donald Cameron, Esq.), the present Cluny (Colonel Duncan Macpherson, C.B.), and the present Glenaladale (Colonel J. A. MacDonald), I could never have identified the places in the mountain fastnesses of Arisaig, Lochaber, and Badenoch. More particularly am I indebted to Glenaladale, who is not only the representative of the Prince's faithful companion during nearly two months of his wanderings, but is the direct descendant of Angus MacDonald of Borradale, the Prince's constant friend and protector. Colonel MacDonald's acquaintance with the traditions of the Prince is as vivid as if the Adventure had happened yesterday, and to his local knowledge I owe the notes which are indicated by the initial [G.].

I have to thank Mr. Alexander Carmichael, formerly of Benbecula, for much help in identifying places and communicating traditions in that island and South Uist; Captain Sidney Williams, R.E., and Mr. John MacIver, Scalpa, for those in Harris and Lewis; Lieut.-Colonel Alexander MacDonald, Portree, for Skye and Raasa; the Rev. Donald M'Lellan, priest of Morar, for Loch Nevis and Morar; the Rev. Roderick Morison of Kintail, for Glenshiel and Strathclunie; Major Grant, Glenurquhart, and Dr. Alexander Ross, Inverness, for Glenmoriston, while to Dr. Ross the Society is further indebted for the sketches of the celebrated cave in Glenmoriston which embellish the volume.

I have to thank the Rev. Colin Mackenzie of Strathglass for much help in tracing traditions and identifying places in the Chisholm country, Glencannich, and Strathglass. To Mr. Alexander Macpherson, Kingussie, and to the Rev. Thomas Sinton of Dores I owe the information about Badenoch and Benalder.

I am indebted to Mr. Chancellor Ferguson of Carlisle and the Rev. S. Whiteside of Shap for traditional information in the north of England; to Mr. R. Bruce Armstrong for that of the Borders; to my father, Professor Garden Blaikie, D.D., for that in the Scottish north-eastern counties; and to Mr. Richard R. Holmes, Her Majesty's librarian, for assistance in verifying some of the Stuart Papers at Windsor.

I desire to acknowledge the help given me by General E. F. Chapman, C.B., Colonel Charles Cunningham, R.E., and Mr. F. T. Hudleston of the Intelligence Division of the War Office, in tracing the Government forces employed in the Expedition; by Mr. Coote and Mr. Henry Jenner of the British Museum in searching for contemporary maps; to the latter I owe thanks for much general assistance; as well as to the Archbishop of St. Andrews, a brother of Glenaladale; to the Roman Catholic clergy in the Highlands; to Mr. John Geddie, and to Mr. Inkson M'Connochie, Secretary of the Cairngorm Club.

In addition, I can only thank generally the town-clerks of nearly every town visited by the Prince in England and in Scotland, the clergy of nearly every parish, and the proprietors of many of the mansion-houses in which he stayed, for communicating traditional information still locally preserved.

In common with all editors of Scottish History Society books, I have experienced untiring courtesy from Mr. Law and his assistants, particularly Mr. Mill, and unlimited help from the resources of the Signet Library.

W. B. BLAIKIE.

The following is a list of the Authorities frequently cited and indicated by Abbreviations.

A.   Information given by the Duke of Atholl from papers in his possession.

A.C.   Atholl Correspondence : Jacobite correspondence of the Atholl Family during the Rebellion. 4to. Abbotsford Club, 1840.

B.H.   Browne's History of the Highlands and of the Highland Clans, including an Appendix of Stuart Papers. 4 vols. Glasgow, 1836.

C.C.   Cochrane Correspondence regarding the affairs of Glasgow, 1745-46. 4to. Maitland Club, 1836.

C.F.M.   Antiquarian Notes, by Charles Fraser-Mackintosh. Second Series : Inverness-shire, Parish by Parish. Inverness, 1897.

C.G.   The Chiefs of Grant. By Sir William Fraser, K.C.B. 3 vols. 4to. Edinburgh, 1883.

C.J.   Chevalier de Johnstone : Memoirs of the Rebellion. 4to. London, 1820.

C.M.   Caledonian Mercury. The Edinburgh Jacobite newspaper in 1745.

C.P.   Culloden Papers. 4to. London, 1815.

C.R.C.   Crofter Royal Commission. Report, Appendix A. Edinburgh, 1884.

D.C.   Duke of Cumberland : A Sketch of his Military Life and Character, as exhibited in the General Orders of H.R.H. 1745-47. By A. N. Campbell-MacLachlan. London, 1876.

D.B.   The Douglas Book, by Sir William Fraser, K.C.B. 4 vols. 4to. Edinburgh, 1885.

D.M.L.   James Drummond MacGregor's Letters, printed in *Blackwood's Magazine* for December 1819.

E.E.C.   Edinburgh Evening Courant. The Government newspaper in 1745.

G.   Information given by Colonel MacDonald of Glenaladale.

G.C.T.   General Cope's Trial : Report of the Proceedings of the Board of General officers on . . . Lieut.-General Sir John Cope, etc. 4to. London, 1749.

G.M.S.   Gartmore Manuscript, printed as Appendix to Vol. ii. of Burt's Letters. 5th Edition. London, 1818.

H.H.   Home's History. The History of the Rebellion in the year 1745. 4to. London, 1802.

H.P.J.   Historical Papers relating to the Jacobite Period. Edited by Col. James Allardyce. 2 vols. 4to. New Spalding Club. Aberdeen, 1895-6.

J.M.B.   John Murray of Broughton : Manuscript Journals and Papers, now being edited for the Society by R. Fitzroy Bell.

L.B.S. Lord Balmerino's Speech on the Scaffold : printed in 'True copies of the papers wrote by Lord Balmerino,' etc. London, 1746.

L.G. London Gazette.

L.G.M. Lord George Murray's Marches of the Highland Army, included in Chambers's Jacobite Memoirs of the Rebellion of 1745. Edinburgh, 1834.

L.L.T. Lord Lovat's Trial : The whole Proceedings in the House of Peers upon the Impeachment, etc. Published by Order of the House of Peers. Fol. London, 1747.

L.M.N. Lord MacLeod's Narrative : contained in the 2nd vol. of Sir William Fraser's 'Earls of Cromarty.' 4to. Edinburgh, 1876.

L.P. Lockhart Papers. 2nd volume. 4to. London, 1817.

L.P.R. List of Persons concerned in the Rebellion. Edited by Lord Rosebery and the Rev. Walter Macleod. Scottish History Society, 1890.

M.C. Mounsey's Occupation of Carlisle in 1745 by Prince Charles Edward Stuart. London and Carlisle, 1846.

M.K. Maxwell of Kirkconnell's Narrative of Charles Prince of Wales's Expedition to Scotland. 4to. Maitland Club, 1841.

N.M'E. Neil MacEachain's Narrative, printed in the *New Monthly Magazine*, November 1840.

M.M'G. Manuscript History of the MacGregors, written about 1830, in the custody of Mr. John MacGregor, W.S.

M.S.L. Memoirs of Sir Robert Strange and Andrew Lumisden, by James Dennistoun. 2 vols. London, 1855.

N.S. Nimmo's History of Stirlingshire. 2nd Edition. Containing extracts from Duncan MacPharic or MacGregor's Manuscript of 1745-6. Stirling, 1817.

R.H. Regimental History (official) of the regiment referred to.

S.C.M. Spalding Club Miscellany. 1st volume: including Bisset's Diary ; Letters to Moir of Stoneywood ; and Marches of the Highland Army, by Captain James Stuart of Ogilvy's Regiment. 4to. Aberdeen, 1841.

S.M. Scots Magazine. When no year is mentioned, reference is intended to the page of the current year of the event.

S.N.M. Scottish National Memorials. Folio. Glasgow, 1890.

References are also made to 'Scotland, State Papers, Domestic, George II.,' from the Record Office, London.

References which are not preceded by initials refer to the three volumes of Bishop Forbes's *The Lyon in Mourning*, to which this book is a supplement.

ITINERARY

[*The dates are Old Style throughout*]

1745

June 22. The Prince embarked at Nantes on board *La Doutelle*, accompanied by the Duke of Atholl (M. of Tullibardine),[1] Sir John MacDonald, Æneas MacDonald, Colonel Strickland, Sir Thomas Sheridan, Captain O'Sulivan, George Kelly, Mr. Buchanan (I. 201, 282), and Anthony Welch, the owner of the ship.[2]

July 4. Joined at Belleisle by the *Elizabeth*, French ship of war, 64 guns [3] (I. 285).

„ 5. Set sail for Scotland (*ib.*).

„ 9. Met the *Lion*, British man-of-war, off the Lizard, which the *Elizabeth* engaged, and was so damaged that she returned to Brest; the *Doutelle* proceeded (I. 203, 286).

„ 22. Sighted Bernera (of Barra) Island (I. 288).

---

[1] William, Marquis of Tullibardine, eldest surviving son of John, first Duke of Atholl; attainted in 1715, during his father's lifetime; was excluded by an Act of Parliament from the succession to the dukedom, which was inherited by his younger brother, James, in 1724. He was always styled Duke by the Jacobite party, and is so designated in the following pages.

[2] The Chevalier Johnstone thus contemptuously describes the party :— ' The Duke of Atholl, attainted and in exile since the year 1715 ; Macdonel, an Irishman ; Kelly, an Irishman, formerly secretary to the Bishop of Rochester; Sullivan, an Irishman ; Sheridan, an Irishman, who had been governor to the Prince ; Macdonald, a Scotsman ; Strickland, an Irishman*; and Michel, his valet-de-chambre, an Italian ; a most extraordinary band of followers ' (C.J. 2).

Æneas MacDonald, in his Examination before the Privy Council, says the expedition was entirely an Irish project.—State Papers Domestic, George II., Jan. 12, 1747/8.

[3] Though a French man-of-war, the *Elizabeth* was fitted out by Walter Rutledge, an Irishman, a merchant of Dunkirk (I. 287).

---

* More likely of the Jacobite family of Sizergh in Westmorland, the head of which followed James II. to France (M.C. 105). Colonel Strickland died in Carlisle three or four days after its surrender to Cumberland (H.P.J. 453).

July 23.   Landed at Eriska Island,[1] and spent the night in a cottage (I. 205, 289).

„ 24.   Visited by Alexander MacDonald[2] of Boisdale (Clanranald's brother), who refused to assist him, or to advise Clanranald to join him; implored the Prince to return, cautioned several chiefs against rising, and prevented Clanranald's islesmen from joining (I. 148, 205, 289; L.P. 440). The Prince persisted, sent a messenger to Sir Alexander MacDonald of Sleat, and Æneas MacDonald went to the mainland to summon his brother, Kinloch Moidart (I. 289).

„ 25.   Sailed to Lochnanuagh and landed at Borradale[3] in Arisaig, the farmhouse of Angus MacDonald (I. 206).

---

[1] The traditional landing-place is on the west side of Eriska—Coilleag a' Phrionnsa (the Prince's Strand). It was conveniently near a house which Boisdale then had at Kilbride in South Uist. On a rocky knoll a little way up from the bay a fleshy-leaved pink convolvulus grows (*Convolvulus major*) which tradition says was planted by the Prince. The ground was enclosed by a stone wall some years ago by Dr. Robert Stewart of Harris (*cf.* C.R.C. *App.* A. 460). The following is from the current number (Jan. 1897) of the *Celtic Monthly* : ' This convolvulus, in spite of many attempts to rear it elsewhere, will only live at Eriskay, and in consequence is known as " the Prince's flower." '

[2] The following are the principal clans of MacDonald, and their cadets or retainers, mentioned in this Itinerary :—

MacDonald of Clanranald.	MacDonald (or MacDonell) of Glengarry.
Boisdale.	Lochgarry.
Kinloch Moidart.	Barrisdale.
Glenaladale.	Scotus.
Morar.	MacDonald of Glencoe.
Borradale.	MacDonald of Sleat (Sir Alexander).
Milton (Flora MacDonald).	Armadale (Flora's stepfather).
MacDonald (or MacDonell) of Keppoch.	Kingsburgh.
Tiendrish (*Ord. Sur.* Tirandrish).	Baleshare.
Tullochcrom.	His brother (Don. Roy MacDonald).

[3] There is considerable discrepancy between the several narratives regarding the exact date of the landing of the expedition. The principal sources of our information upon this point are four in number : (1) The narrative of Duncan Cameron, a retainer of Lochiel's, sent from France with the Prince to pilot the party on their arrival in the Western Islands (I. 201). (2) The account of Æneas MacDonald, the banker of Paris, and brother of Kinloch Moidart, who also accompanied the Prince from France (I. 281). (3) The MacDonald chronicler of the Lockhart Papers, a member of the Clanranald clan, one of the Prince's earliest adherents, and the first person to whom he gave a commission in

July 25.   Remained in the neighbourhood of Borradale either on shore or on board ship until August 10th.

The day following the landing, Kinloch Moidart, who had arrived, was sent south to summon John Murray of Broughton, the Duke of Perth (J.M.B.), and Lochiel. Young Clanranald, Alexander MacDonald of Glenaladale, Æneas MacDonald, and the Lockhart chronicler (a Clanranald MacDonald), visited the Prince on board ship (L.P. 479). Young Clanranald and Allan Mac-

---

Scotland (L.P. II. 483). And, lastly (4), two letters of the Prince himself written to his father, which are printed in Lord Mahon's *History* (vol. iii. app. pp. xxiv-v). Cameron says they reached Eriska '*about*' July 21st' (I. 204). Æneas MacDonald says they reached it on the 23rd, and emphasises the date by stating they had been 'eighteen days at sea from July 5th,' the day of leaving France (I. 288). Both state, or at least imply, that the ship sailed to Borradale after the interview with Boisdale at Eriska, that the Prince landed there on the 25th of July, which Cameron emphasises by calling it St. James's Day (I. 206), a more likely date to be remembered than a mere day of the month. The Lockhart chronicler also states that the actual going ashore took place on that day (L.P. II. 482); but he had previously stated that the party had anchored in Lochnanuagh Bay on the 18th, and he describes several interviews that took place on board ship. After the landing the material discrepancies in the narratives cease. That Bishop Forbes sifted Cameron's story and believed it correct in the main as supplemented by Æneas MacDonald's, is evident from his conversation with Alexander MacDonald (I. 352, 353). The dates of Æneas MacDonald might at first sight be assumed trustworthy, as he was an educated man of business, and one of the Prince's companions, and was returning to his own birthplace and the home of his family; yet some doubt is thrown on his accuracy by his mis-statement of the place of his brother's visit, and he is twice corrected in his facts by Bishop Forbes (I. 289 *n*, 351, 352), though it is quite probable that these were the mistakes not of the banker but of Dr. Burton in reporting him. The Lockhart chronicler states that on landing on the 25th the *Doutelle* at once weighed anchor and returned to France (L.P. 482). That this was not the case is evident from the Prince's letter of 4th August, old style, on which day the ship was on the point of leaving. Æneas MacDonald also states that on the 26th they coasted about the isles between Skye and Mull, and landed some of their passengers (I. 290), and he quotes the *Gazette* for corroboration (S.M. 1745, 396). That the party had not then abandoned the ship is borne out by the Prince himself, whose letters to his father are dated, '*abord du vaisseau le dutellier, à l'ancre dans la Baie de Loughaylort, le 2 août, V.S.,*' and '*Loughaylort, August 4, O.S.,* 1745.' (The names of the ship and of the place seem to have been misread by Lord Mahon's transcriber.) Loch Aylort is not far from Lochnanuagh and Borradale, but this shows that the Prince was not all the time on shore in the early days of August. That the dates in the Lockhart Papers cannot be entirely trusted is shown by the fact

July 25.   Donald (brother of Kinloch Moidart) were sent to
                  Skye to summon Sir Alexander MacDonald and
                  MacLeod of MacLeod (L.P. 481), and Glenaladale
                  was sent to assemble Clanranald's clansmen as a
                  guard for the Prince. MacDonald of Scotus, on
                  behalf of Glengarry, MacDonald of Keppoch,
                  MacDonald of Glencoe (*ib.*), and Hugh Mac-
                  Donald, brother of Morar (III. 50), also visited the
                  Prince. All, even those who had accompanied
                  him from France, implored the Prince to return;
                  'the Prince was single in his resolution of landing'
                  (III. 51). On Clanranald's return from Skye with
                  a refusal from Sir Alexander and MacLeod,[1] he too
                  was so disheartened that he was reluctant to go on,

that the raising of the standard is dated August 9th, while it undoubtedly took
place ten days later.

The probability is that the members of the party were all more or less in a
state of excitement. Events moved so quickly, and so much had happened
between the time of landing and of writing the narratives, that exact dates and
the sequence of events were not accurately remembered. There seems little
doubt that the Lockhart chronicler confused July 25th, the date of the Prince's
first going on shore, which was the marked day always remembered, with
August 4th, the day that he finally abandoned the ship; and that the chronicler
counted back from the former date instead of from the latter when arranging his
experiences in writing. There seems no doubt that from July 25th to August 4th
the Prince was sometimes on shore, and sometimes on board ship. The interviews chronicled in the Lockhart Papers must have taken place after, not
before, the 25th of July. See also additional note, p. 83.

[1] MacLeod immediately communicated the news of the Prince's arrival to Lord
President Forbes in a secret letter, dated 3rd August. In his postscript he
writes : 'Young Clanronald has been here with us, and has given us all possible
assurances of his prudence' (C.P. 203-4). Both MacLeod and Sir Alexander
MacDonald joined the Government side.

Although MacLeod of MacLeod declared for the Government, many of the
clan went out with the Prince, notably Bernera, Muiravonside, Raasa, Glendale,
Brea. I have been unable to trace from contemporary sources when and where
they joined the Prince, or how they were brigaded. None of the plans of the
battles printed in Home's *History* show MacLeods on the field, but a very
incorrect plan of the Battle of Culloden, printed in the *Scots Magazine* for 1746,
p. 217, and frequently copied in other books, shows a battalion of MacLeods,
100 strong, on the left centre of the first line, between the MacIntoshes and the
MacLeans, who were brigaded with the MacLachlans; and a map of the same
battle by John Finlayson, in the British Museum, places the battalion between
the MacLeans and the Chisholms. Home in a note states that MacLeod of
Raasa and his men joined the Prince at Stirling (in January), and formed part of
Glengarry's Regiment at Falkirk and Culloden (H.H. 249).

July 25.

but he was persuaded to join,[1] and at once raised his clan (III. 52).

Lochiel[2] sent his brother, Dr. Archibald Cameron, to urge the Prince to return, whereupon the Prince sent young Scotus to Achnacarie 'to persuade Lochiel to do his duty,' upon which Lochiel came to Borradale (*ib.*).[3] Lochiel, after vainly persuading the Prince to abandon his enterprise, agreed to raise his clan[4] on condition of the Prince giving security for the full value of his estate should the attempt prove abortive, and on MacDonald of Glengarry undertaking in writing to raise his clan for the Prince, which he did, under command of his second son, Angus, and his kinsman Lochgarry (III. 120, 121).[5]

[1] This was no doubt the moment of the dramatic scene described by Home, when the Prince, turning from Clanranald to young Ranald MacDonald a brother of Kinloch Moidart, exclaimed, 'Will you not assist me?' 'I will,' he replied, 'though no other man in the Highlands should draw his sword.' . . . Without further deliberation, the MacDonalds agreed to go on (H.H. 39, 40).

[2] The 'Lochiel' of the Forty-five was Donald Cameron, the eldest son of John Cameron of Lochiel, chief of Clan Cameron, whom Lord MacLeod mentions as being appointed, jointly with himself, commander-in-chief of the reinforcements that marched from Perth towards Stirling in December 1745 (L.M.N. 387). Father and son were in Strathspey with the Prince in Feb. 1746 (C.G. II. 236).

[3] Home tells how John Cameron of Fassefern, Lochiel's brother, on whom he called on his way to Borradale to pay his respects to the Prince and to give his reasons for declining to join him, advised Lochiel not to see him, for 'if this Prince once sets his eyes upon you he will make you do whatever he pleases' (H.H. 44 *n*).

[4] Murray of Broughton states (in his Manuscript Journal) that Lochiel 'did not hesitate one moment to answer the summons, but repaired thither immediately and assured him of his readiness to join him with his followers.' Murray, however, did not join the party till three weeks later, when details of incident might have been forgotten or not communicated to him. The evidence of Lochiel's reluctance to go out is incontrovertible.

[5] Glengarry himself did not go 'out,' but shortly afterwards joined Cope at Crieff (G.C.T. 16). His eldest son, Alexander [? Pickle the Spy], had been sent in May to France with a message from several of the Highland chiefs, desiring the Prince not to make an attempt at that time without foreign assistance. In France he missed the Prince, who meantime set out for Scotland. Young Glengarry, on returning, was taken prisoner and confined in the Tower until after Culloden (III. 120; also *History of the MacDonalds*, by Alex. Mackenzie, Inverness, 1881). Angus MacDonald, the 'young Glengarry' of the expedition, was accidentally killed at Falkirk after the battle. In spite of his caution the old chief was imprisoned in Edinburgh Castle shortly after Culloden, and was not released until October 1749 (S.M. 1746, p. 392; 1749, p. 459).

July 25.   Arrangements were then made to raise the
                    standard of James VIII. at Glenfinnan on Monday,
                    August 19th (L.P. 480).

> *Aug.* 1. *Proclamation by Government of a reward of
> £30,000 to any person seizing the Prince on his landing
> in the British Dominions* (L.G. Aug. 3).

Aug 4.   The frigate *Doutelle,* having discharged its stores and
                    armaments, left Lochnanuagh and went privateer-
                    ing (I. 293),[1] and the Prince took up his quarters at
                    Borradale.   Here he continued to send messengers
                    and letters to his friends and adherents all over
                    the country.[2]   Clanranald's people alone were his
                    guard at Borradale (L.P. 482).

> *On August 8th, the first news of the Prince's landing
> reached Cope in Edinburgh, and he at once arranged to
> collect stores and assemble an army at Stirling* (G.C.T. 7).[3]

„ 11.   The Prince, with artillery and baggage, went by sea
                    to Kinloch-Moidart (I. 207, 292) skirting the heads
                    of Lochnanuagh and Loch Aylort, while Clan-
                    ranald's clansmen marched by the shore (L.P. 483).

„ 11-17.   The Prince remained at Kinloch-Moidart [4] (I. 292).

> *On August 13th Lord President Forbes went to Inver-
> ness, where he rallied to the Government side the Lords
> Sutherland and Reay (MacKay), the Grants of Grant, the
> Munros, Sir Alexander MacDonald, MacLeod of MacLeod,*

---

[1] The Prince sent away the ship as soon as he conveniently could, in order to
cut off all possibility of retreat (J.M.B.).

[2] Some of these letters exist.   One to the Earl of Cromarty who afterwards
joined him, which is facsimile'd in Sir William Fraser's *Earls of Cromarty* (I.
ccxii), is given here as a specimen.   It is in the handwriting of Sir Thomas
Sheridan, but signed and addressed by the Prince himself.

                              BORADEL, *August ye 8th,* 1745.

' Having been well inform'd of y[r] Principles and Loyalty, I cannot but express
at this juncture, that I am come with a firm resolution to restore the King, my
Father, or perish in y[e] attempt.   I know the interest you have among those of
y[r] name, and depend upon you to exert it to y[e] utmost of y[r] Power.   I have
some reasons not to make any application to y[e] Earl of Seaforth without y[r] advice,
w[ch] I therefoir desire you to give me sincerely.   I intend to set up the Royal
Standard at Glanfinnen on Monday y[e] 19th instant, and shou'd be very glad to
see you on that occasion.   If time does not allow it, I still depend upon your
joyning me with all convenient speed.   In y[e] meantime, you may be assured of
the particular esteem and friendship I have for you.   CHARLES, P. R.'

[3] Cope's forces.   See additional note, p. 90.

[4] Burnt down by Cumberland's soldiers, May 1746 (S.M. 287).

Aug. 11.-17.   *Lord Fortrose (Seaforth MacKenzie), and others, raising twenty companies for Loudon's regiment among Highlanders who might otherwise have followed the Prince* (C.P. 370 et passim).

„ 14.   Captain Switenham of Guise's regiment, when on his way from Ruthven to take command at Fort-William, taken prisoner by Keppoch's people, within twelve miles of the fort (G.C.T. 19, I. 352).

„ 16.   First outbreak of hostilities. MacDonald of Tiendrish (of Keppoch's clan) assisted by some of Glengarry's men, attacked and took prisoner on the shores of Loch Lochy[1] two companies of the Royal Scots who were marching from Perth to reinforce the garrison of Fort-William (I. 36, L.P. 483).

„ 18.   Joined by John Murray of Broughton at Kinloch-Moidart[2] (J.M.B.; S.M. 1747, p. 107). The Prince marched to Loch Shiel and went by boat to Glen-aladale, where he spent the night. Joined by Gordon of Glenbucket, who brought Captain Switenham with him (J.M.B.).

„ 19.   The Prince went by boat to Glenfinnan at the head of

---

[1] The fight began at High Bridge and finished at Laggan[achdrom], at the head of the loch (L.P. 483).

[2] The chronicler of the Lockhart Papers says, that Murray joined the Prince at Glenaladale or Glenfinnan (L.P. 441); but Murray himself distinctly states that he joined at Kinloch-Moidart before the Prince left it. In his evidence at Lord Lovat's trial he states that he tried to persuade the Prince to abandon the enterprise (S.M. 1747, 108); but in his Journal there is nothing of this after the actual landing; on the contrary, he gives an account of his vigorous preparations and arrangements. He says he was informed of the Prince's arrival by an anonymous letter, received at Broughton, Peeblesshire, apparently sent by the Duke of Perth or by Kinloch-Moidart, who had joined the Duke. Before this he had had manifestoes printed in Edinburgh, to be ready for the rising. He at once set out and joined Kinloch-Moidart at Arnprior in Perthshire. Thence he sent a secret emissary to the Lord Advocate and Sir John Cope at Edinburgh, with false intelligence artfully mingled with truth with a view of breaking up the garrisons in the Highlands (J.M.B.). This emissary was Rob Roy's son, James MacGregor or Drummond, the father of R. L. Stevenson's heroine, Catriona (Stuart Papers, B.H. III. 84; H.H. 289). Maxwell of Kirkconnell, however, states that Murray had written to Sheridan, expressing his surprise that the Prince had come alone, and advising his return, and that Sheridan had replied that it was owing to the encouragement Murray had given, that the Prince had come in this particular way; and upon the receipt of this letter Murray at once started to join (M.K. 21); but this statement must be received with caution.

Murray's dates occasionally differ slightly from Cameron's, which are followed here.

Aug. 19.　Loch Shiel.　He was guarded by fifty Clanranalds and was met by Morar with 150 of Clanranald's clan (L.P. 484).　The Stewart standard was raised by the Duke of Atholl (i. 207, etc.), Captain Switenham, the prisoner, looking on (J.M.B.).　In the afternoon the Prince was joined by Lochiel with 700 Camerons, and later by Keppoch with 300 Mac-Donalds (L.P. 484, etc.).　The Prince spent the night in ' a little barn at the head of the loch ' (J.M.B.).

„ 20.　Remained at Glenfinnan while the arms and baggage were carried from Loch Shiel to Loch Lochy (L.P. 442).

„ 21-22.　At Kinlochiel.[1]　Here he learned that Sir John Cope was marching by Dalwhinny towards Fort Augustus.　Switenham was dismissed on the 21st and joined Cope at Dalnacardoch on the 25th (G.C.T. 19).　The Prince, hearing for the first time of the reward of £30,000 offered for his capture, prepared a counter proclamation [2] offering £30 for the capture of George ii. (J.M.B.), afterwards altered to £30,000 (S.M. 1747, p. 626).

„ 23.　At Fassefern,[3] the house of John Cameron,[4] Lochiel's brother (i. 207).

„ 24.　Marched to Moy,[5] crossing a hill to avoid a ship of war lying off Fort-William (i. 207).

„ 25.　At Moy (i. 207).　Murray of Broughton this day named Secretary (J.M.B.).

„ 26.　Marched to Letterfinlay [6] and on to Invergarry

---

[1] A letter from the Prince, dated Kinlochiel, 22nd August, to Sir James Grant of Grant is facsimile'd in Sir William Fraser's *Chiefs of Grant*, i. 386.

[2] There is no old house now with which the Prince's name is associated, but a flat moor is pointed out where the reward for King George was publicly proclaimed.

[3] Fassefern still stands, but two years ago the rooms occupied by the Prince were considerably altered.

[4] John Cameron did not join the Prince.

[5] The house occupied at Moy no longer exists.

[6] Cameron states that the Prince spent the night at Letterfinlay (i. 207), but from the united evidence of Murray's Journal, the Lockhart Papers (L.P. 442), and the indirect evidence of the Culloden Papers, it is pretty certain that he went on the same day to Invergarry.

The Prince's halting-place at Letterfinlay is believed to be the old inn on Wade's road, now sometimes used for changing post-horses.

Aug. 26.   Castle.[1] Met at Invergarry by Fraser of Gortleg,
with a message from Lord Lovat[2] assuring the Prince
of his services, and urging him to march north
through Stratherrick to Inverness, when the Frasers
would rise, and probably the MacLeods, Sir Alexander MacDonald, the MacKenzies, the Grants, and
MacIntoshes. The Duke of Atholl, on the other
hand, pressed him to push south and raise the
Atholl country, and reach Edinburgh as soon as
possible to unite his followers there. The latter
proposal was adopted (L.P. 442). Here a document was drawn up and signed by all the chiefs
present, pledging themselves not to lay down their
arms or make peace separately without consent of
the whole (J.M.B.).

Joined by the Stewarts of Appin under Ardshiel,
260 men (L.P. 442). Heard that Cope was at
Dalwhinny preparing to march over Corryarrack.
Sent part of the army by a forced march to seize
the pass before Cope could reach it (I. 207, L.P.
443, etc.).

*On Aug. 19th Cope left Edinburgh for Stirling; 20th,
marched to Crieff with the following force: five companies of Lee's, Murray's regiment, two companies of Lord
John Murray's Highlanders, and was joined at Crieff by
eight companies of Lascelles's (G.C.T. 16). Marched to
Amombrie [Amulree], 22nd; Taybridge [Aberfeldy], 23rd;
Trinifuir, 24th; Dalnacardoch, 25th; Dalwhinny, 26th
(ib. 45). Before leaving Edinburgh he strengthened the
garrisons of Edinburgh, Stirling, Glasgow, and Inveraray,
and left Gardiner's dragoons to defend the Forth at Stirling,
and Hamilton's dragoons to defend Edinburgh (ib. 16).*

„ 27.   Marched to Aberchalder (L.P. 442).[3] Joined by
400 Glengarry MacDonalds, the MacDonalds of
Glencoe (120 men, H.H. 117),[4] and some of the

---

[1] Glengarry himself had gone to join Cope. See *ante*, p. 5, *n* 5. Invergarry
Castle was burned down by Cumberland's soldiers in May 1746 (S.M. 287).

[2] This was Lord Lovat's first communication to the Prince (J.M.B.).

[3] This house no longer exists.

[4] Home states that one-half did not join until the army was between Perth
and Dunblane (H.H. 77 *n*).

Aug. 27.　　　Grants of Glenmoriston (J.M.B., L.P. 442), but
　　　　　　　deserted by some of Keppoch's men.[1]

　,, 28.　　　　Marched over the Corryarrack Pass to Garvemore
　　　　　　　(L.P. 443). Here, to his disappointment, the Prince
　　　　　　　found that Cope, having learned he had seized the
　　　　　　　pass, avoided meeting his army, and had turned
　　　　　　　north, marching by Ruthven towards Inverness.
　　　　　　　Anxious to fight Cope, it was proposed, at a hurriedly
　　　　　　　summoned council, to go through Strathdearn by
　　　　　　　forced marches and intercept him at Sliochmuick
　　　　　　　(*Ord. Sur.* Slochd Mor); but it was decided that
　　　　　　　Cope had too long a start and that their own men
　　　　　　　were too fatigued to make success certain (J.M.B.).

　　　　　　　Against the Prince's wish (J.M.B.) a small party
　　　　　　　was sent to Ruthven under O'Sullivan and Dr.
　　　　　　　Cameron to destroy the barracks there, but were
　　　　　　　beaten off with loss by the garrison (I. 294).

　　　　　　　A party of Camerons was sent from Garvemore to
　　　　　　　seize MacPherson of Cluny[2] at his own house; he
　　　　　　　was carried prisoner to the Prince next day on the
　　　　　　　march to Dalwhinny (L.P. 440, C.P. 391).

　,, 29.　　　　Marched to Dalwhinny (I. 353).[3]

　　　　　　　*On August 26th, Cope at Dalwhinny, learning that the
　　　　　　　Prince had occupied the Corryarrack Pass, determined to
　　　　　　　avoid him and march for Inverness. Reached Ruthven,
　　　　　　　27th; Dalrachny, 28th; Inverness, 29th (G.C.T. 47).*

---

[1] Murray of Broughton states that the reason for the desertion was a private
quarrel with the chief, which in his MS. is explained by a note to have been the
refusal of the chief, a strict Protestant, to allow a favourite priest to accompany
the clan, many of whom were Catholics. I am informed, however, by Mrs.
Macdonnell of Keppoch, whose late husband was great-grandson of the Keppoch
of the '45, that this must be a mistake, as the chief was never a Protestant, though
his eldest son married a Protestant wife and abandoned his religion.

[2] Ewan MacPherson, younger of Cluny, the eldest son of Lauchlan MacPherson, was Lochiel's first cousin and Lord Lovat's son-in-law, and it is a doubtful
point, whether or not he was an unwilling prisoner. He had been gazetted to a
company of Lord Loudon's regiment on June 8th (S.M. 298), and had been in
attendance on Sir John Cope and Lord Loudon until the day before his capture,
when he had left Ruthven to raise his clan for the Government. He had been
insultingly treated by Cope, and 'an angel could not resist the soothing close
aplications of the rebels' (C.P. 412). He was detained prisoner until the Prince
reached Perth (J.M.B.).

[3] Tradition says the Prince slept this night in the heather.

Aug. 30. Marched to Dalnacardoch[1] (I. 208, 294). Here Lochiel sent home 150 of his men who were imperfectly armed (J.M.B.).

„ 31. Marched to Blair Castle[2] in Atholl, the seat of the Duke of Atholl (I. 208, 294). Joined by Col. John Roy Stewart[3] (J.M.B.).

[About] this day the barracks of Inversnaid were surprised by the MacGregors and 89 soldiers made prisoners (C.M. Sept. 3, G.M.S. 352).

On Aug. 31st King George II. arrived in London from Hanover (L.G. Aug. 27-31).

Sept. 1. At Blair. Joined by Lord Nairne and his brother, Mercer of Aldie (A.). Roy Stewart sent north 'to manage the Grants' country and raise what men he could' (J.M.B.).

„ 2. The Prince went to the House of Lude[4] (I. 208).

„ 3. Marched to Dunkeld[5] (I. 208).

„ 4. Dined at Lord Nairne's[6] house (*ib.*), entered Perth in the evening, and proclaimed James VIII. (L.P. 443).

„ 4-10. Remained at Perth.[7] Joined here by the Duke of Perth,[8] Lord George Murray, Lord Ogilvy, Hon. Wm. Murray, Laurence Oliphant of Gask, Lord Strathallan, the Chevalier Johnstone, and others

---

[1] Dalnacardoch was then a public-house on Wade's road (II. 134). A new inn was built by Government in 1774; it is now a shooting-lodge of the Duke of Atholl.

[2] There is no traditional 'Prince Charles's Room' in Blair Castle. As Duke James (brother of the Jacobite Duke William) and his successor, who was the son of Lord George Murray, both adhered to Government, their inclination would be rather to hush matters up than to keep alive traditions. There is a state bed at Blair, purchased in 1700, which it is believed was used by the Prince (A.).

[3] He had been a British cavalry officer either in the Scots Greys or Gardiner's Dragoons (H.P.J. II. 368).

[4] The old House of Lude no longer exists. A new house was built 1826-30.

[5] The Prince occupied Old Dunkeld House, belonging to the Duke of Atholl: it was pulled down about 1830. The present house was formerly an inn (A.).

[6] Nairne House, in Strathord, about eight miles from Dunkeld, was entirely demolished about the end of the eighteenth century (A.).

[7] Traditionally the Prince occupied Lord Stormont's house, where the Union Bank now stands.

[8] James Drummond, grandson of James, 4th Earl of Perth, who was created Duke by James II. at St. Germains. He was always termed Duke of Perth by the Jacobites, and is so called in these pages. Lord John Drummond was his brother.

Sept. 4-10.   (J.M.B., M.K. 31, C.J. 10). Lord George Murray [1] and the Duke of Perth appointed Lieutenant-Generals (C.J. 12), O'Sullivan, quarter-master-general, and Sir John MacDonald, formerly an officer of Carbineers, instructor of cavalry (M.K. 32). Keppoch and Clanranald sent to Dundee, proclaimed James VIII., collected some public money, captured two ships, and returned to Perth (L.P. 486).

On the 10th the Prince visited Glenalmond to inspect some of his new troops assembled by the Duke of Perth, including MacGregor of Glencairnaig and forty of Glengyle's MacGregors (N.S. 545).

Robertson of Struan joined with 200 men [2] (M.K. 33). Cluny was released and went home to raise his clan (J.M.B.), which he undertook to do on receiving the Prince's security for the value of his estate (III. 121).

At Perth the Prince received assurances of help from France and Spain.[3]

The Prince, having received intelligence that Cope had sent to Edinburgh to order shipping to be collected at Aberdeen to transport his army to the Firth of Forth, held a council to consider if it would not be best to march quickly north and intercept Cope on his march to Aberdeen. It was decided that the army should march south as rapidly as possible and take possession of Edinburgh (J.M.B.).

Cope left Inverness and reached Nairn Sept. 4th, Elgin 5th, Fochabers 6th, Cullen 7th, Banff 8th, Turriff 9th, Old Meldrum 10th; arrived at Aberdeen Sept. 11th (G.C.T. 33; S.M. 1895, p. 301).

„ 11.   The Prince visited Scone; breakfasted at the House of Gask [4]; dined at Tullibardine [5] (Lord George

---

[1] It is interesting to note that Lord George had been appointed a Sheriff-Deputy, and had actually visited Cope at Crieff on Aug. 21 (G.C.T. 16, 132). A letter to Lord Advocate Craigie, written after this visit, pooh-poohs the rising. It is printed in Mr. Omond's *Lord Advocates of Scotland*, II. 15. Edinburgh, 1883.

[2] Home says there were only 100 Robertsons (H.H. 117). Cf. additional note, p. 91.

[3] See additional note, p. 84 *n.*

[4] The old house, now a ruin, was pulled down about 1800.

[5] Now entirely demolished.

Sept. 11.' Murray's). Marched to Dunblane [1] (1. 209). Here the Duke of Perth brought up 150 men (M.K. 33).[2]

„ 12. Marched to Doune [3] (1. 209).

„ 13. Crossed the Forth at the Fords of Frew or Boquhan. 'The Young Chevalier had been the first who put foot in the water and waded thro' the Forth at the head of his detachment' (C.M. Sept. 16). The Prince at Leckie House,[4] and the army encamped at Touch (L.P. 489). From Leckie House the Prince wrote to the Provost of Glasgow demanding a contribution of £15,000 from the city, and that all arms should be given up (C.C. 105.)

On the appearance of the Highlanders at the ford, *Gardiner's dragoons retired to Linlithgow* (L.G.M. 35).

„ 14. Marched by Stirling, where they were entertained by the Provost, but fired at by the garrison of the castle (1. 209) and St. Ninians; halted at Bannockburn, where the Prince dined with Sir Hugh Paterson, and went on to Falkirk. The Prince spent the evening at Callander House (Earl of Kilmarnock's),[5] and the troops encamped in Callander Parks (J.M.B.). At night Lord George Murray (M.K. 33), with Lochiel, Keppoch, Glengarry and Ardshiel, started for Linlithgow to attack the dragoons in their camp, but found they had previously retreated [6] (A.C. 15, L.G.M. 36).

---

[1] By tradition he occupied Balhaldie-Close, a house in Dunblane then belonging to MacGregor of Balhaldie; still occupied, and the tradition preserved.

[2] Maxwell of Kirkconnell, who, however, only joined the Prince at Edinburgh, says that these and Struan's 200 men were the first reinforcements received since leaving Glengarry, and presumably the only ones (M.K. 33). Perth's detachment comprised some MacGregors, including Glencairnaig (N.S. 545). Home states that Glengyle joined with 255 MacGregors at Conagan near Dunblane [*Ord. Sur.* Conichan is really in Glenalmond] (H.H. 77), but this is contradicted by the evidence of MacPharic, corroborated by Graham of Gartmore (G.M.S. 351, N.S. 700). See also additional note, p. 92.

[3] Tradition still points out the rooms in Newton House in which the Prince was entertained by the Edmonstone family.

[4] Leckie then belonged to George Moir. The old house still exists.

[5] The old mansion, replete with historical associations, still stands.

[6] An interesting fact is mentioned by Murray alone, that the Prince after supper, and a pretended retirement to bed, with great secrecy headed a force of 500 men to take the dragoons in flank. He marched to the Ford of Avon, which

Sept. 15 (Sunday). Reached Linlithgow at 6 A.M. and took possession of it.   The army encamped to the east of the
town; the Prince requested the magistrates to
hold church services as usual, which the minister
did not do; prevented his men from entering the
town; and spent the day quietly in Linlithgow
Palace.   In the evening the army bivouacked three
miles to the east of the town on the Edinburgh
road, the Prince sleeping in an adjacent house.[1]
All the officers from Lord George Murray down-
wards slept beside their men, 'without other covering than their plaids' (J.M.B.).

    „   16.   Marched through Winchburgh and Kirkliston, halting
for two hours at Todshall,[2] whence he sent out
a reconnoitring party.   In the afternoon he
advanced to Corstorphine.

> *Gardiner's dragoons retreated to Coltbridge, a mile west
> of Edinburgh, where they were joined by Hamilton's
> dragoons from Leith.   On the approach of the Highland
> army both regiments fled by Leith and Musselburgh to
> Haddington.*

From Corstorphine the Prince sent a summons
to the magistrates demanding the surrender of
Edinburgh.   His army turned south and encamped
at Slateford, in Colinton parish, the Prince quarter-
ing at Gray's Mill[3] in the house of the miller.

---

is a mile and a half above the bridge (not half a mile as Murray says), close to
Muiravonside, the home of his A.D.C., MacLeod; there he learned that the
dragoons had retreated.   A tradition preserved in the district, that he visited
Muiravonside House, is the only corroboration of Murray's story I have found.
The visit to Muiravonside, which still stands, could only have taken place on this
occasion, and it seems likely enough that he halted there for refreshments in the
early morning.

Lord George Murray, when writing to his brother on the 15th, informing
him of the capture of Linlithgow, makes no mention of this adventure of the
Prince (A.C. 15, L.G.M. 36).

[1] Traditionally Champfleury, then called Kingscavil.   A new house occupies
the old site.

[2] *Anglicè* 'Foxhall,' which is the name of the modern mansion on the old site.

[3] Gray's Mill, formerly a flour mill, is now a paper mill, on the Water of Leith
a little below Slateford, and still bears the old name.   The house adjoining
the mill occupied by the Prince is now a farmhouse, and his room, a very small
one, is still pointed out.

Sept. 16.　During the night a deputation was sent by the magistrates to the Prince to ask for time, which was refused, and the deputies returned to Edinburgh.[1] Joined by Lord Elcho.

„　17.　After the departure of the civic deputation a party of 900 men was sent under Lochiel, accompanied by Murray of Broughton and O'Sullivan (J.M.B.), to seize the city. They marched in the dark by Merchiston and Hope Park to the Netherbow gate (where the High Street now joins the Canongate). The accident of the opening of the gate to allow the exit of the carriage that had carried back the deputation permitted Lochiel to rush in, overpower the city guard, and make himself master of the city ; the regular troops had retreated to the castle, the dragoons had fled to Haddington, and the volunteers had been disbanded. This took place in the early morning in broad daylight (ib.).

At noon the Prince, with the main body of the army, marched by Prestonfield and the King's Park into Edinburgh. The Prince went in triumph to Holyrood, and the army encamped in the King's Park. The heralds, pursuivants, and trumpeters were secured by the advance guard, and in their robes of state they proclaimed James VIII. and Charles Prince Regent, at the Market Cross, ' betwixt twelve and one o'clock.' The castle, commanded by General Guest, did not surrender.

„　18.　The Prince at Holyrood, the army in the King's Park. Joined by MacLachlan of MacLachlan and his clan, 150 men (II. 209), and by Lord Nairne (M.K. 39), with 250 men from Athole.[2] A drum beat up for volunteers, when several entered the Duke of Perth's regiment (J.M.B.)

„　19.　The army moved to Duddingston, leaving guards only at Holyrood. Hearing in the evening that

---

[1] Contemporary accounts of the negotiations and of the capture of Edinburgh will be found in most of the narratives of the Expedition and in the *Caledonian Mercury*, the *Edinburgh Evening Courant*, and the *Scots Magazine*, from which sources these events have been abstracted without constant references.

[2] The numbers are taken from Home's *History*, App. p. 331, *n.*

Sept. 19.

Cope had marched to Haddington, the Prince, resolving to meet him, rejoined the army at Duddingston and ordered the guards to follow in the morning (J.M.B.).

Cope left Aberdeen by sea, September 15th; arrived at Dunbar, 17th; was joined there by Gardiner's and Hamilton's dragoons; marched to Haddington, 19th; and to Prestonpans, 20th (G.C.T. 48).

„ 20.

Joined by Grants of Glenmoriston[1] (C.M., 23 Sept). Putting himself at the head of the army and sending forward all his cavalry (50 horse) as an advance guard (J.M.B.), the Prince marched by Musselburgh to the brow of Carberry Hill, by Falside Castle through Tranent, and lay all night on the high moorland to the east of that village. Cope had formed his army on the low ground between the sea and the high road half-way between Prestonpans and Cockenzie, and south of these villages. The Prince slept on the field, 'laying on the ground without any covering but his plaid' (*ib.*).

„ 21.

THE BATTLE OF PRESTONPANS OR GLADSMUIR.[2]—At three in the morning the Highlanders marched down towards the sea, crossed a morass, and formed line of battle to the east of Cope. 'In seven or eight minutes' the battle was over. Cope's infantry was all either killed, wounded, or taken prisoner, and many of the Highland prisoners enlisted with the Prince.[3] The Prince spent the night at Pinkie House;[4] the army occupied Musselburgh.

The Prince sent messages to the Presbyterian clergy to continue their services the next day,

---

[1] Part of the clan had joined him on August 27th. The total number could not have exceeded 100 (H.P.J. I. 172).

[2] The battle was generally called GLADSMUIR by the Jacobites. A quaint petition of the inhabitants of Prestonpans complains that they are 'deprived of that honour and fame which of right belongs to them,' and demands that the battle should have its title from one of the towns or villages near which it was fought, and not after 'a barren muir' (S.M. 521). Since then it has been generally called the Battle of PRESTON, and more modernly of PRESTONPANS.

[3] Descriptions of the battle are in all the contemporary narratives and journals.

[4] Pinkie House then belonged to the Marquis of Tweeddale; the old house still stands, and a 'Prince Charles's Room' is shown.

Sept. 21.   Sunday, as usual, which permission, with two excep-
tions, was not exercised [1] (J.M.B., C.M. Sept. 23,
S.M. 441).

After the battle, the question of marching at once to
Berwick was discussed, but was abandoned, as it was felt
that the army was too small to keep the communications
open with Edinburgh and the north, while if the Prince
made some stay in Edinburgh, his friends would have
time to rise, the army could be organised, reinforcements obtained from the north, and assistance might be
expected from France, since the Prince had given proof of
his having a strong party in Scotland (J.M.B., M.K. 43).

*Cope, with the cavalry, fled by Lauder to Coldstream, and
the next day to Berwick (G.C.T. 43).*

,, 22.   The Prince returned to Holyrood, where he remained
until October 31st. The army marched into Edinburgh, and was at first billeted in the city and
suburbs. Lochiel volunteered to take the guard
in the Lawnmarket over the castle gates, to prevent any sally from the castle, and his regiment
bivouacked in the Parliament House (L.G.M. 45)
and the Tron Church (J.M.B.).

The Prince despatched an agent to England to summon
his friends to join him (C.P. 226). [2]

A council was formed, which daily assembled at
Holyrood. [3]

---

[1] The Prince was particular in sending such messages. His army was very
regular in attending divine service. While at Derby, when a battle was expected,
many officers and men took the sacrament (L.G.M. 76).

[2] Hickson, who was arrested at Newcastle on the 27th.

[3] The Council comprised the Duke of Perth, Lord Lewis Gordon, Lord George
Murray, Lords Elcho, Ogilvie, Pitsligo, and Nairne, Lochiel, Keppoch, Clan-
ranald, Glencoe, Lochgarry, Ardshiel, Sheridan, O'Sullivan, Glenbucket, and
Murray of Broughton. Lord George Murray in a letter to his brother gives
a different list, including the Duke of Atholl, President ; Earl of Wemyss, Lords
Strathallan, Arbuthnot, Kenmure, and Cardross, Sir James Stewart of Good-
trees, Wauchope of Niddry, Hamilton of Boag, MacLeod of Muiravonside,
Stirling of Keir, Graham of Airth, and Lord Provost Stewart (A.C. 25). Lord
George's list seems to be the names of people they hoped to get ; the first list,
Lord Elcho's, those who actually attended. Faction, which had begun at Perth,
early showed itself in the Council between the French-Irish and the Scots members,
and especially between Lord George Murray and John Murray of Broughton,
whose side the Prince espoused. The strife continued increasingly to the end

Sept. 24.   Alexander MacLeod, of Muiravonside, advocate, sent
            to Skye to summon Sir Alex. MacDonald, MacLeod
            of MacLeod, and MacKinnon of MacKinnon, his
            credential [1] stating that the Prince had positive
            assurance of assistance from France and Spain.[2]
            Kinloch-Moidart, Fraser of Dulcraig, and Mac-
            Donald of Barrisdale were sent with a similar
            message to Lord Lovat (J.M.B., etc.).

  „   26.   Hay of Restalrig sent to Glasgow [3] to enforce the
            demand for a contribution of £15,000 requisitioned
            from Leckie, which was compromised for £5000 in
            cash and £500 in goods (C.C. 123, L.G. Oct. 5-8).
            Kelly sent to France with despatches (J.M.B.).

            A few days after the occupation of Edinburgh all the
            troops except the guards on the castle and on Holyrood
            were removed to a camp at Duddingston, with outposts
            in some of the villages. The Prince daily visited
            Duddingston to review his troops,[4] and occasionally

---

of the Expedition (cf. Lord Elcho's Narrative quoted in Scott's *Tales of a
Grandfather*, lxxix, and Maxwell of Kirkconnell, 54). For further light on the
relations between the Prince and Lord George Murray, see the letters printed in
Appendix, p. 73.

[1] The letter is printed in Home's *History*, App. xviii.

[2] 'French and Spanish assistance,' see additional note, p. 83.

[3] Although John Murray says that 'the Chevalier took care that the party
should be so inconsiderable as might plainly evince to the Inhabitants that he
did not intend to have it by force, but in freindship,' yet claymores seem to have
been present. In M.M'G. there is a quotation from what is stated to be a
'Declaration upon oath by Andrew Cochrane, Esq., Provost of Glasgow, at the
Bar of the House of Commons,' which I have not had the opportunity of
verifying: 'That soon after the battle of Preston, viz. 26th Sept^r, John Hay,
Writer to the Signet, came to Glasgow with a party of horse, and was met there
by Glengyll, Chief of the M'Gregors, with a great part of that Clan.'

[4] 'Abundance of people, friends as well as enemies, had made it their business
to find out the real numbers of the Prince's army, but to no purpose ; great pains
had been taken to conceal its weakness. Though the Prince was almost every
day reviewing some of his men, he never made a general review. There were
always troops at Leith, Musselburgh, or some villages adjacent, when he reviewed
the camp, besides the garrison that remained constantly in the city, and, lest
people should reckon them in their different cantonments, they were eternally
shifting their quarters, for no other reason than to confound the over-curious.
This uncertainty as to the strength of the Prince's army, and the general pre-
sumption that it was much stronger than it really was, made the Court of England
very cautious and slow in sending Wade to Scotland, and gave the Prince abundance of time to assemble and form his army' (M.K. 53).

Sept. 26.   spent the night in his tent among them (J.M.B., M.K. 45).

„ 29.   The Prince, with a view to prevent provisioning ordered all communication with the castle to cease. General Guest[1] retorted by a letter to the magistrates, threatening to cannonade the town if this were enforced (C.M. Sept. 30).

„ 30.   The Prince replied, threatening full reprisals if this were done (*ib.*).

Oct. 1.   The garrison of the castle fired on the town and did some damage (*ib.* Oct. 2).

„ 2.   The Prince issued a proclamation permitting communication with the castle by special pass (*ib.*).[2]

„ 3.   Joined by Lord Ogilvy (600 men, H.H. 128), Farquharson of Monaltrie[3] (30 men, H.P.J. ii. 480), Viscount Dundee (Graham of Duntrune) at the head of several gentlemen from Angus (C.M. Oct. 4).

„ 4.   Joined by Gordon of Glenbucket, with 400 men,[4] from Banff and Aberdeenshire, chiefly Grants and Farquharsons; by Colonel David Tulloch and John Hamilton, afterwards Governor of Carlisle, with 480 men from Strathbogie and Enzie (*ib.* Oct. 7).

„ 6.   Joined by a body of Camerons and MacDonalds of Keppoch (*ib.*).

„ 9.   Joined by Lord Pitsligo with 132 horse and 248 foot from Aberdeen and Banffshire (*ib.* Oct. 9).

> *Oct. 10th. A reward of £50,000 proclaimed in Ireland for capture of the Prince dead or alive* (L.G. Oct. 15-19).

----

[1] Sir Walter Scott (*Tales of a Grandfather*) ascribes this letter to General Preston, but the *Caledonian Mercury* (Sept. 30) distinctly states that the letter was written by Guest.

[2] An interesting account of the remarkable relations between the Castle and Holyrood during the Prince's occupation of Edinburgh, by John Campbell, assistant secretary of the Royal Bank, is printed in the *Miscellany* of the Scottish History Society (vol. xv.), Edinburgh, 1893.

[3] Monaltrie did not accompany the Prince to England. He was at the skirmish of Inverurie on Dec. 23, and joined the Prince at Bannockburn in January.

[4] This is printed 1400 in the *Caledonian Mercury*, apparently a misprint for 400. The *London Gazette* of Oct. 12th states that Ogilvy and Glenbucket's united forces amounted to 700. Maxwell calls Glenbucket's force 300. The 600 here assigned to Lord Ogilvy is taken from H.H. 128.

Oct. 11.   Joined by Gordon of Aberlour and Steuart of Tinnin-
                nar, with two companies of foot from Banffshire
                (C.M. Oct. 11).

> *Oct. 11th, Lord Loudon, who had fled with Cope from*
> *Prestonpans to England, returned to Inverness and took*
> *command of the forces the Lord President had been raising*
> (L.G. Oct. 26-29).
>
> Oct. 12th. A treaty made between Marquis d'Argen-
> son, for Louis xv., and Colonel O'Brien, the Chevalier's
> agent in Paris, by which the King undertook to assist
> the Prince and to send troops to defend the provinces
> that had submitted to him [1] (*dated Oct. 23 New Style*).

„ 12-13.   Joined by Hon. Charles Boyd (Kilmarnock's son[2]) with
                a body of gentlemen, Gordon of Buckie and Gordon
                of Glastirum, with tenants; by the Chief of Mac-
                Kinnon and his clan (120 men, J.M.B., C.M. Oct. 14).

„ 14.   Du Boyer, Marquis d'Aiguilles, titular French ambas-
                sador, arrived at Holyrood [3] (C.M. Oct. 16).

                The camp of Duddingston broken up, and the
                troops moved to the city and suburbs [4] (S.M. 492).

---

[1] This treaty is printed in the Stuart Papers, B.H., App. xvi.

[2] Called brother in C.M. Apparently a mistake.

[3] The French ambassador, at first received with effusion, became an object of
suspicion to the Jacobites as time went on and French assistance, so eagerly
expected, did not arrive. His credentials were doubted, and he was even
suspected of being a spy. Murray of Broughton states, however, that 'he had a
short credential from the French king to the Pretender's son,' and again, 'The
Marquis d'Aiguilles, at Carlisle, showed his instructions to this examinant,
which were pretty long: that the purport of them was to learn, as particularly as
possible, the situation of things in Scotland, the strength of the Pretender's army,
what friends he had, and what he would be able to do; and to send an exact
account of it to the French ministers; and that if things looked favourable for
the Pretender they would assist him with troops, etc.'—State Papers Domestic,
George II.: Examination of John Murray of Broughton, Aug. 13, 1746.

[4] An idea of how the troops were cantoned in Edinburgh may be got from the
following order of the day given by Captain James Stuart of Lord Ogilvy's
regiment, whose itinerary of the march of the Lowland part of the Prince's army is
printed in the *Miscellany* of the Spalding Club, vol. I.: 'Tuesday, 15 Oct.
Glengarry continues in the town and Canongate. Wednesday—Lochyell at the
ports [gates] of the town and Canongate. Thursday—Lord Ogilvy has the
town; Glenbucket the Canongate. Friday—Duke of Perth the town and
Canongate. Saturday—Keppoch the town, and Duke of Athole the Canongate.
Saturday, clan Ronald the town and the ffoot come with Lord Pitsligo, and
David Tulloch the Canongate. Collonel Stuart to be constantly quartered at
the town, beyond Jockis Lodge, and to relieve his own guard. The guards that

Oct. 15.   Joined by Lord Lewis Gordon; by the Master of Strathallan, with 300 men from Balquhidder (C.M. Oct. 16).

,, 18.   Joined by the Earl of Kilmarnock, the Earl of Niths- dale, and Viscount Kenmure [1] (*ib.* Oct. 21).

Joined also in Edinburgh by the Earl of Kellie (in- ference), the Hon. Arthur Elphinstone [2] (L.B.S. 3), and by Maxwell of Kirkconnell. [3]

Two troops of Life Guards were organised in Edinburgh, one under Lord Elcho, [4] and another, originally intended for Lord Kenmure, was given to Lord Balmerino (J.M.B.) A regiment of hussars was also raised (S.M. 493).

Oct. 17. General Handasyde arrived at Berwick (L.G. Oct. 19-22).

Oct. 19. The Duke of Cumberland arrived in London from Flanders (L.G. 15-19).

Between Oct. 9th and 19th four ships from France landed at Montrose and Stonehaven, with artillery and stores, bringing over among others Du Boyer and James Grant, the engineer. These stores were escorted to Edinburgh by the Duke of Atholl's men and the Mac- Phersons. They were ferried across the Forth at Alloa, where batteries were erected on both sides of the river to secure the passage against English cruisers (C.M. Oct. 11-25).

,, 24.   Joined by 100 MacGregors from Balquhidder (*ib.* Oct. 25).

On Oct. 1st George II. ordered a strong force of cavalry and infantry to prepare to march to Scotland under Marshal Wade (L.G. *Sept. 28-Oct. 1). They assembled at Doncaster about the 19th, and reached Newcastle the 29th* (S.M. 489). [5]

---

are relieved take possession of the quarters of those they are relieved by. Glen- garry the guard in town; Lochyell in Lieth; Athole, Ardsheal, and M'Lachlan in Duddistown ; Keppoch and M'Kinnen at Inch; Duke of Perth at Restelrigg; Clan Ronald at Newhaven ; the north country ffoot in Mercer's house at Lieth.'

[1] Both Nithsdale and Kenmure ran away the following day (J.M.B.).

[2] He became Lord Balmerino on the death of his brother, Jan. 5, 1746 (S.M. vol. vii. p. 594).

[3] Inference from Stuart Papers (B.H. App. xxv.).

[4] 'Lord Elcho had, with great diligence, compleated it all of gentlemen of familly and fortune, and tho they did not amount to above a hundred, yett I may say there never was a troop of better men in any service . . . and all extreamly well mounted' (J.M.B.).

[5] 'Wade's Army,' see additional note, p. 94.

Oct. 24.   *The English army in Flanders, recalled to England, began*
to arrive in the Thames on Sept. 23rd, and continued coming
over until Dec. 1st (L.G. *Sept.* 22-*Dec.* 1). *Troops were*
also sent to Newcastle and Berwick, and by the 29th seven
battalions British and some Dutch troops had landed there
(L.G. *Oct.* 29).

„ 28.   Rev. Alex. Gordon, S.J., sent to France with despatches.[1]

„ 29.   Joined by MacPherson of Cluny in advance of his clan
(C.M. Oct. 30).

'Towards the end of October,' finding Lovat still
evasive, and Sir Alexander MacDonald and MacLeod
recalcitrant; that the public money was not sufficient
to pay the army, and private contributions were at an
end; fearing, too, that inaction in Edinburgh would
debauch his troops, who were constantly deserting, and
learning that Wade was on his way north, the Prince
determined to march into England (J.M.B., M.K. 54).

Before leaving Edinburgh Lord Strathallan was appointed to command the force gathering at Perth,
with Oliphant of Gask as his lieutenant; MacGregor of
Glengyle was made Governor of Doune Castle, to watch
Stirling Castle, which still held out for the Government
(J.M.B.); David Fotheringham (I. 210, L.P.R. 212)
was made Governor of Dundee, Moir of Lonmay Governor of Aberdeen (S. C. M. 355), Carnegie of Balnamoon
Governor of Montrose (III. 20).[2] Lord Lewis Gordon
had previously gone north as lord-lieutenant to raise
the Duke of Gordon's followers (S.C.M. 401, M.K. 51),
and young Glengarry went back to the Highlands to
raise more MacDonalds (L.P. 472).

Some time in October a body of MacLeans,[3] which

---

[1] This date may be New Style, *i.e.* 17th. Gordon's report is printed in the
Stuart Papers, B.H. App. xxv. It is inaccurate and misleading, but is valuable
as reflecting the talk and expectations of the party. Here is one sentence:
' Quant à l'Angleterre, on y est prêt à Le recevoir à bras ouverts et à se déclarer
ouvertement pour Lui dèsqu'il paroitra en force et soutenu par la France.'

[2] Murray of Broughton mentions these appointments, but leaves the names
blank. They are filled in from other sources.

[3] I have been unsuccessful in finding from contemporary sources when and
where the MacLeans joined the Prince. Tradition says that they joined under
MacLean of Drimnin during the retreat from Stirling. There were 182 MacLeans
at Culloden brigaded with the MacLachlans under the chief of MacLachlan,
' seeing their chief was not there' (II. 209). This battalion of MacLachlans
and MacLeans is shown in Home's and other contemporary plans of the battle.
MacLean of Brolus joined the Government side (S.M. 1746, p. 141).

Oct. 29.   was marching to Edinburgh to join the Prince, was attacked, disarmed, and dispersed by Lieutenant-Colonel Campbell of Loudon's regiment (L.G. Oct. 29-Nov. 21).

,, 30.   The Duke of Atholl with 600 men, and the artillery and gunners from France under James Grant,[1] director of ordnance, joined the army (C.M. Nov. 1).

At a council of war the question of the march into England was discussed. The Prince favoured an advance on Newcastle, which Wade had reached the day before with tired troops, not much more numerous than his own (the Dutch who had been sent there were prevented by the capitulation of Tournay from fighting against the French, and their allies); an advance on Carlisle would give the appearance of shunning Wade, who, besides, might march across country and oppose his passage of the river Esk. Lord George Murray and the Highland chiefs favoured an advance on Carlisle, to avoid the risk of a battle, and to give his English adherents time to join him. The council separated without coming to a conclusion (J.M.B., M.K. 58).

,, 31.   The Prince, without abandoning his own opinion, announced his concurrence with Lord George Murray's scheme (*ib.*).

To mask his intentions it was agreed that the army should divide in two columns, one to march by Peebles and Moffat, and the other by Lauder and Kelso, thus threatening the road to Newcastle, the columns to unite near Carlisle (J.M.B., M.K. 59).

Joined by Cluny MacPherson's clan (400, C.M. Oct. 30).

The army concentrated at Dalkeith. The Prince spent the night at Pinkie House (II. 115, C.M. Nov. 1).

About the beginning of November, Glengyle, who had made a recruiting raid into Cowell, Argyleshire, was defeated by Colonel Campbell with the Argyleshire Militia (L.G. Nov. 23-26).

---

[1] James Grant (or Grante) was a French artillery or engineer officer. He is always spoken of with respect. The Chevalier Johnston calls him an officer of great talent (C.J. 59). It was he who made the map referred to by Bishop Forbes (II. 377), and cf. additional note, p. 104.

Nov. 1.   The Prince marched to Dalkeith.[1] The army was
          divided into two columns.[2]

          One under the Dukes of Atholl and Perth, consisting
          of the Lowland troops, Atholl Brigade,[3] Perth's,
          Ogilvie's, Glenbucket's and Roy Stewart's regiments,
          the artillery, and the Perth horse (*i.e.* Kilmarnock's),
          marched to Auchindinny[4] (J.M.B., M.K. 61).

  „ 2.   The Prince's column, with Lord George Murray as
          second in command, consisting of the clans and the
          rest of the horse, halted at Dalkeith (II. 116, 192).

  , 3.   The Prince's column marched to Lauder,[5] the Prince
          on foot at the head of the clans (M.K. 61) 'with
          his target over his shoulder' (S.M. 493).

  „ 4.   The Prince rode back to Channelkirk to bring up
          stragglers, and then marched to Kelso[6] (J.M.B.).

  „ 5.   Halted at Kelso (II. 117). A body of cavalry under
          Ker of Graden[7] sent across the Tweed scouted
          towards Wooler in Northumberland to create the
          impression that the army was advancing to New-
          castle-on-Tyne (J.M.B., M.K. 61).

  „ 6.   Crossed the Tweed and marched to Jedburgh[8] (II. 117.)

---

[1] The Prince is understood to have lodged at Dalkeith Palace, the Duke of
Buccleuch's, but no 'Prince Charlie's Room' is now shown. The family is said
to have been absent.

[2] The journals of the day mention a third column taking a middle route
(S.M. 529). It probably comprised impedimenta and followers, as it is not
mentioned by either of the military writers, Lord George and Kirkconnell.

[3] Lord George Murray's own battalion accompanied him (A.).

[4] For the details of the march of this column, see Captain Stuart's (of Ogilvy's)
narrative quoted before. It marched by Auchindinny, Peebles, Broughton,
Tweedsmuir, Moffat, and Lockerby, and joined the Prince's column at Newton of
Rowcliff in England (S.C.M. 290).

[5] The Prince lodged in Thirlestane Castle (Earl of Lauderdale's), and occupied
the north room behind the billiard-room, since known as Prince Charlie's room.
The castle was not occupied at the time, and bedding, etc., had to be brought
from an inn in the town, since demolished (MS. in possession of the Lauderdale family).

[6] The tradition is that the Prince lodged at Sunlaws, three miles south, on the
Jedburgh road. The house (property of Major Scott Kerr) has been burned
down three times since 1745, and the only relic of the Prince is a white rose,
known as Prince Charlie's Rose, originally planted by him, which has been
preserved by cuttings to the present day.

[7] A.D.C. to the Prince (I. 360).

[8] The Prince occupied, traditionally, the house now 9 and 11 Castlegate,
then the property of Ainslie of Blackhill.

Nov. 7.		The Prince marched with the clans by the Rule valley to Haggiehaugh,[1] on the south side of the Liddel. The cavalry were sent by Hawick and Langholm (M.K. 62).
,,	8.	Crossed the Esk into England, and spent the night at Reddings.[2] They were rejoined near Longtown by the cavalry (ib.).
,,	9.	Marched towards Carlisle. Joined by the Duke of Atholl's column, which had marched that day from Lockerby, at Newtown of Rowcliff; crossed the Eden, and encamped in the villages to the west of Carlisle. The Prince lay at Muirhouse,[3] two miles west of Carlisle (II. 117, 192).
,,	10.·	Carlisle, which was garrisoned by the Cumberland and Westmorland Militia (L.G. Nov. 9-12), summoned to surrender; the deputy-mayor[4] refused, and a battery was begun to the north-west of the Penrith gate. The troops not in the trenches were quartered in neighbouring villages, and the Prince lay the night at Blacklehall[5] (II. 117, 192 n), where, getting intelligence that Marshal Wade was about to march from Newcastle-on-Tyne to relieve Carlisle, he determined to give him battle at Brampton, where the ground was mountainous, and best suited for his troops (J.M.B.).
,,	11.	The troops recalled from the trenches, and the whole army marched to Brampton[6] (II. 117, J.M.B.).
,,	12.	Encamped at Brampton (II. 117).
,,	13.	The Prince, finding that Wade was not approaching, sent back half the army to Carlisle to continue the

---

[1] Haggiehaugh is the old name of Larriston, where tradition and relics of the Prince's visit survive.

[2] A farmhouse then tenanted by David Murray (M.C. 41). The house has been rebuilt, and no tradition of the visit appears now to survive.

[3] Now Moorhouse Hall.

[4] Thomas Pattinson; the Mayor, Joseph Backhouse, 'being a mere cypher' (M.C. 4).

[5] Blackwell Hall, one mile south of Carlisle, the property of Sir Richard Musgrave.

[6] The Prince's lodging is believed to be a house in High Cross Street, now or lately occupied by Mr. Hetterington, draper. It is recorded that on the 13th the Prince went to Warwick Bridge, and dined with Squire Warwick. (See *Brampton in* 1745.)

Nov. 14.   siege, which was planned by Lord George Murray, and intrusted to the Duke of Perth (J.M.B.).[1]

> *Nov. 13. The Lord Justice-Clerk, the judges and principal Government officers, who had fled on the Prince's approach, returned in state to Edinburgh* (S.M. 538).

The Prince at Brampton. The siege of Carlisle continued. A white flag displayed in the evening (II. 193).

> *On the 14th Handasyde, with Price's and Ligonier's foot and Hamilton's and Ligonier's (formerly Gardiner's) Dragoons, arrived in Edinburgh, and were shortly afterwards sent to Stirling to guard the passes of the Forth* (L.G. Nov. 16-19, S.M. 538-540).

„ 15.   The Prince instructed Murray of Broughton and the Duke of Perth to arrange terms, and the town and castle both surrendered. The commandant (Colonel Durand) and the garrison were dismissed to their homes (J.M.B., L.G. Nov. 19-23).

> Lord George Murray, taking umbrage at the arrangements for capitulation being taken out of his hands, and representing that the fact of the Duke of Perth's being a Roman Catholic operated against the Prince's interest in England, resigned his commission as Lieutenant-General, but at the wish of the army resumed it, upon which the Duke of Perth resigned his lieutenant-generalship, and reverted to the command of his own regiment (J.M.B.).

The Prince remained at Brampton (II. 118, 192).

„ 16.   The Prince at Brampton (*ib.*).

> *Nov. 16. An army of five regiments of cavalry and fifteen of infantry ordered to march to Lancashire under Sir John Ligonier* (L.G. Nov. 12-16).

„ 17.   The Prince and his column entered Carlisle (II. 118, 192).

---

[1] It is interesting to note John Murray's commendation of Lord George Murray's military talents here. He says, 'the blocade was formed by one-half of the army under L.G.M., and the disposition left to himself, which he performed with so much judgement that the few French officers then in the Army allow'd they had never seen anything of the kind better executed, and regreted that a man possessed of so fine a natural genious for war should not have been bred a Solger' (J.M.B.). Lord George, however, *was* bred a soldier; he served from 1712 to 1715 in the 1st Royals, when he deserted and joined Lord Mar (A.). The *Caledonian Mercury*, quoted in S.M. 532, gives the credit of the siege operations to Grant.

Nov. 17.   *Marshal Wade left Newcastle on the 16th and reached Hexham on the 17th, when, hearing that Carlisle had fallen, and finding the roads almost impassable on account of snow, he returned to Newcastle on the 22nd* (L.G. Nov. 22 and 26).

,, 18-20.   The Prince at Carlisle, in the house of Mr. Highmore,[1] attorney (II. 120). On the 18th, at a council of war, the alternatives were discussed: to march against General Wade: to return to Scotland: to await events at Carlisle and see if the English Jacobites would rise: to march through Lancashire towards London. The last was resolved on, partly to remove all possible pretext from the Jacobites of Lancashire (the stronghold of Jacobitism) for neglecting to join the cause (J.M.B., L.G.M. 48, etc.).

         MacLachlan of MacLachlan was sent to Lord Strathallan at Perth to call up the re-inforcements (II. 209).

,, 21.   Marched to Penrith [2] (II. 120, 193).

,, 22.   Halted at Penrith (*ib.*).

         Nov. 22nd. In compliance with the treaty of Oct. 12th (23rd), Lord John Drummond landed with a force of about 800 men[3] at Montrose, Stonehaven, and Peterhead, composed of his own (French) regiment of Royal Scots and a piquet of 50 men from each of the six (French) Irish regiments, under Brigadier Stapleton (L.G. Nov. 30-Dec. 5, L.M.N. 384, etc.)

         Drummond at once sent messengers to Count Nassau, who commanded the Dutch auxiliaries at Newcastle, requiring him to retire from the strife, in terms of the capitulation of Tournay, which after negotiation he was obliged to do (S.M. 588).[4]

,, 23.   Marched to Kendal[5] (*ib.*).

---

[1] In English Street, known as the Earl's Mansion, the property of the Earl of Egremont. The house has been divided into two and refronted, and one of the two lately rebuilt. The Prince's visit is recorded on the front.

[2] The Prince lodged in what was then the George and Dragon Inn, now or lately the shop of Mr. Ramsay, chemist (*History of Penrith*, 1858).

[3] Two of Drummond's transports were taken by English cruisers. Lists of the officers captured are printed in the *London Gazette*, Nov. 26-29 and Dec. 7-10.

[4] Dutch and Hessian troops, see additional note, p. 88.

[5] The Prince stayed at a house in Stricklandgate, now called Stricklandgate House, occupied by Mr. W. B. Thompson, printer.

Nov. 24.   Halted at Kendal. Being Sunday, service was held
            in the churches, and attended by all the people of
            rank in the army, both Protestants and Catholics.
            The Prince himself ' could not goe, there being no
            churchman of higher rank than the curate then in
            the place' (J.M.B.).

            Nov. 24. The *Hazard*, English sloop-of-war, captured
            in Montrose harbour (III. 20, L.G. Dec. 5).

,,   25.   Marched to Lancaster[1] (II. 120, 193).

,,   26.   Marched to Preston[2] (*ib.*). This being the farthest
            that the Highlanders had been able to penetrate
            to in England in 1648 and 1715, Lord George
            Murray marched the army at once across the
            bridge over the Ribble to remove any superstitious
            fear that Preston was again to be their goal
            (J.M.B.).

,,   27.   Halted at Preston. The Prince was here joined by
            Mr. Townley, Counsellor Morgan, and Mr. Vaughan[3]
            from Wales, and 'some few common people, but
            no numbers as was expected' (*ib.*).

,,   28.   Marched to Wigan[4] (II. 121, 193).

            *Wade's army left Newcastle-on-Tyne Nov. 24th, reached
            Persbridge 28th* (L.G. Nov. 23-26, 26-30, S.M. 534).

            Ligonier becoming ill (M.K. 72), *the Duke of Cumber-
            land was appointed to command his army, and joined it at*

---

[1] The Prince lodged in Mrs. Livesay's house, Church Street, now the Con-
servative Club.

[2] The entry to Strait Shambles was formerly called Mitre Court, and in premises
on the north side, long occupied as the *Preston Journal* office, tradition says the
Prince made his lodging (Hardwick's *History of Preston*, 1857, p. 231).

[3] This was William Vaughan (H.J.P. II. 450). His elder brother, Richard,
of Courtfield (then in Monmouthshire, now in Hereford), also joined the Prince,
was an officer in Perth's regiment, and fought at Culloden. He was great-great-
grandfather of the present Cardinal-Archbishop. William was excluded from
the general pardon of 1747, and both brothers entered the Spanish service
(Burke's *Landed Gentry*). The other two English gentlemen who joined at
Preston, Francis Towneley and David Morgan, were both executed on July 30,
1746. Towneley was of Towneley Hall in Lancashire ; and Morgan who was
titularly the 'Prince's Counsel,' came from Monmouthshire (cf. I. 43, H.P.J.
II. 373, 448, and S.M. 1746, pp. 320-327).

[4] The Prince is supposed to have slept in the Old Manor House in Bishops-
gate, close to the Parish Church, still in existence, the property of the Rector of
Wigan.

Nov. 28.   *Lichfield on the 27th Nov. The army was then cantoned from Tamworth to Stafford, with the cavalry at Newcastle-under-Lyme* (L.G. Nov. 26-30).

,,   29.   Marched to Manchester[1] (II. 121, 193).

,,   30.   Halted at Manchester (*ib.*). Here the Prince was joined by a considerable number, whom, along with the Preston recruits, he formed into 'the Manchester Regiment' of not more than 300 men,[2] and gave command to Townley, who had been formerly an officer in the French service (J.M.B., C.J. 50). These were practically the only English Jacobites that joined the Prince.[3]

At Manchester a retreat was informally talked of, as there had been no rising in England as was expected, and no landing of a French force as had been hoped. Lord George Murray thought they might make a further trial and go the length of Derby, where, if there was not greater encouragement, he would propose a retreat (M.K. 70).

Dec. 1.   Marched to Macclesfield[4] (II. 122); the Prince with the troops by Cheadle, the artillery and train by Gatley (L.P. 457). Hearing that the Duke of Cumberland was at Lichfield, with his forces in the neighbouring towns, a council of war was held, in which it was agreed to push on by forced marches so as to get between the Duke and London.[5]

To mask the intention, Lord George Murray took a column to Congleton, on the road to Newcastle-under-

---

[1] The Prince lodged in John Dickenson's house, Market Street Lane. It was afterwards the Palace Inn, and subsequently 'Palace Buildings.' It is unlikely that any portion of the old house is now standing (cf. Axon's *Annals of Manchester*, p. 84; John Byrom's *Remains*; Hibbert-Ware's *Foundations of Manchester*).

[2] Probably considerably less. There were only 114 made prisoner at the surrender of Carlisle, where the regiment were left in garrison. See p. 34, *n*6.

[3] 'During the whole time of their being in England they received no application or message from any persons in England, which surprised and disappointed them extremely.'—State Papers Domestic, George II.: Examination of John Murray of Broughton, Aug. 13, 1746.

[4] The Prince occupied a house in Jordangate, in which the Duke of Cumberland also stayed when in pursuit. Since then it has been called Cumberland House. The house is at present occupied and retains the name.

[5] See Hay of Restalrig's account, printed in Home's *History*, App. xxxii.

Dec. 1.   Lyme and Lichfield, which forced the Government troops to retire to Stone. He then turned to his left, marched through Leek to Ashburne, and thence to Derby, where he was joined by the Prince on the 4th (L.G.M. 53, 54).[1]

,,   2.   Halted at Macclesfield (II. 121).

,,   3.   Marched to Leek[2] (*ib.*)

,,   4.   Marched to Ashburne (*ib.*), and on to Derby (L.P. 458), the advance-guard going as far as Swarkston Bridge (L.G. Dec. 3-7).

      The Prince entered Derby in the evening, and lodged in the house of Lord Exeter[3] (S.M. 616, L.G. Dec. 9, etc.).

,,   5.   Halted at Derby. Learning that Wade was at Wetherby, Cumberland at Lichfield, and a third army assembling on Finchley Common to protect London, at a council of war a retreat was resolved on, to the great mortification of the Prince, who 'could not prevail upon one single person'[4] to join him. Lord George Murray agreed to command the rear-guard (L.G.M. 55).

      Cumberland was at Stafford on Dec. 2nd, Stone 3rd, Stafford 4th, Lichfield 5th, and his army at Meriden Common and Coventry 6th (S.M. 574).

      Wade was at Wetherby Dec. 5th, and on the 8th with his infantry at Ferrybridge, his cavalry having advanced to Doncaster (L.G. Dec. 7-10).

,,   6.   BLACK FRIDAY. The Retreat begun. Marched to Ashburne[5] (M.K. 79, L.G. Dec. 9).

---

[1] Lord George Murray says that they reached Derby on the 5th. Though he is seldom wrong, this must be a mistake. The other contemporary authorities state that the Prince arrived in Derby on the evening of Wednesday the 4th, which the *London Gazette Extraordinary*, Dec. 9, corroborates by inference.

[2] Traditionally the Prince occupied an old house on the north side of the Market Place, the birthplace of Thomas Parker, Lord Chancellor, first Earl of Macclesfield. A small room is still shown as the Young Chevalier's room.

[3] Lord Exeter's house was in Full Street. It was pulled down about forty years ago, and a street made through the gardens.

[4] The Prince's own words (H.H. 340).

[5] Gibb's dates are slightly departed from here, and occasionally elsewhere during the march, and those given by other contemporary authority are substituted. The discrepancies are, however, more apparent than real. Gibb's dates are taken from his cash book, and he would no doubt sometimes pay on the evening of

Dec. 7.   Marched to Leek (II. 122, 194).

„   8.   Marched to Macclesfield (*ib.*).

„   9.   Marched to Manchester (*ib.*).

„   10.   Marched to Wigan (*ib.*).

„   11-12.   Marched to Preston, and halted a day there (*ib.*).

> The Duke of Perth was sent with a cavalry escort to call up reinforcements from Scotland. He was driven back at Shap, and obliged to rejoin the army at Penrith. (L.G.M. 59-61, L.P. 495, S.M. 577.)

„   13-14.   Marched to Lancaster, and halted a day there (*ib.*), to show that he was retiring and not flying, and would fight if attacked (M.K. 82).

> *Cumberland,[1] with all his cavalry and 1000 foot, including mounted infantry, left Meriden in pursuit on the 8th, reached Macclesfield on the 10th* (L.G. Dec. 7-14).
>
> *Wade, intending to intercept the Prince, reached Wakefield on the 10th, where, finding himself outgeneralled by three or four days' march, he sent on his cavalry under General Oglethorpe to pursue, while he returned to Newcastle-on-Tyne* (*ib.* Dec. 10-14).
>
> *Oglethorpe's cavalry joined Cumberland at Preston 13th* (*ib.* Dec. 14-17).
>
> *Cumberland's infantry not employed in the pursuit began to return to London* (*ib.* Dec. 19).

„   15-16.   Marched to Kendal, and halted a day (II. 122, 194).

„   17.   Marched to Shap[2] (*ib.*).

> *Cumberland was at Wigan the 14th, Lancaster, 16th, Kendal, 17th* (L.G. Dec. 19), *where his advance-guard overtook the Prince's rear-guard at Clifton* (*ib.* Dec. 17-21).

„   18.   Marched to Penrith (II. 123, 194). In the evening Lord George Murray and the rear-guard were attacked by a body of Cumberland's cavalry and dismounted dragoons, whom they beat off, and made

---

arrival and sometimes on the morning of departure. Gibb has no entries for Ashburne on the retreat, but the accounts in Kirkconnell's narrative and the *London Gazette Extraordinary* leave no doubt that the Prince spent the night of the 6th at Ashburne. A room in Ashburne Hall is still pointed out as his lodging.

[1] Cumberland's Army, see additional note, p. 94.

[2] The Prince is believed to have stayed in what was then the inn. It is on the west side of the main road, half way up the village, now divided into two houses, occupied by Mr. Hudson and Mrs. Rigg. The tradition is preserved that the Prince complained of being overcharged.

Dec. 18.   good their retreat at the SKIRMISH OF CLIFTON[1]
                  (II. 86).

          After the skirmish Cumberland spent the night at Clifton,
          halted at Penrith till all his forces joined him on the 20th
          (L.G. Dec. 21-24).

„ 19.   Marched to Carlisle (II. 123). Here the Prince
          received despatches from Lord John Drummond
          and Lord Strathallan, with encouraging accounts
          of the army they had collected, and promises
          from France of succour, of which the few troops
          and artillery already sent were but an earnest to
          enable the Prince to reduce the Scottish for-
          tresses. King Louis desired the Prince to avoid
          any decisive action until these succours should
          arrive (M.K. 87).
              A council of war was held[2] (at which Lord George
          Murray was not present, L.G.M. 74) in which it
          was resolved to march to Scotland, and unite with
          the army collected there (M.K. 87).
              The Prince, who never abandoned his designs on
          England, in order to facilitate his re-entry into
          that kingdom, left a garrison of about 400[3] men,
          including the Manchester Regiment, and several
          French and Irish officers. Townley was left com-
          mandant of the town, and John Hamilton governor
          of the castle (*ib.* 88).

„ 20.   THE PRINCE'S BIRTHDAY.[4] The army forded the Esk
          and divided into two columns; Lord George Murray
          with the Lowland regiments, making a feint to-
          wards the Edinburgh road, marched that night to

---

[1] A plan of the ground is given by Chevalier Johnstone, and accounts of the
skirmish by him and by Lord George Murray, Maxwell of Kirkconnell, and
both the Lockhart chroniclers. Johnstone's account gives, evidently by mistake,
the credit of the defence to Lochiel instead of to Cluny (C.J. 61).

Chancellor Ferguson of Carlisle, to whom I am indebted for most of the
traditional notes of the halting-places in Cumberland and Westmorland, has
contributed to the *Trans. Cumberland and Westmorland Antiq. Soc.*, 1889, an
exhaustive memoir on the retreat through Westmorland, illustrated with a series
of maps, including a contemporary one of the Skirmish of Clifton. A letter
from a quaker farmer of Clifton describing the action is printed in his appendix.

[2] So Kirkconnell says, but cf. Appendix, p. 74.   [3] See p. 34, *n* 6.

[4] Often called December 31st, which is the date according to New Style.

Dec. 20.   Ecclefechan, while the Prince with the Highlanders and cavalry went to Annan [1] (L.G.M. 74, M.K. 89).

Lord George Murray's column marched by Lockerby to Moffat, Douglas and Hamilton, arriving in Glasgow on the 25th, one day in advance of the Prince (S.C.M. 315).

„ 21.   The Prince marched to Dumfries [2] (II. 124).

„ 22.   From Dumfries the Prince issued an order to the army, in which he assured them that the King of France had promised to send a powerful army (S.C.M. 312). Marched to Drumlanrig, and lodged in the castle [3] (II. 124).

„ 23.   Marched up Nithsdale, then turned up the Menock Pass by Leadhills to Douglas. The Prince lodged in Douglas Castle [4] (*ib.* L.P. 499).

On Dec. 3rd Loudon marched a force through Stratherrick to relieve Fort Augustus, threatened by the Frasers under the Master of Lovat (S.M. 589). On the 11th he took Lord Lovat (who had been corresponding with both sides) a prisoner to Inverness, whence he escaped on the 20th, and at once the clan marched under the Master to join the Prince's army (L.L.T. 45). At the same time Loudon sent a strong force under MacLeod of MacLeod, Munro of Culcairn, and Grant of Grant to relieve Aberdeen [5] (II. 344, S.M. 589).

Dec. 23rd. Lord Lewis Gordon marched from Aberdeen, and completely defeated MacLeod at the SKIRMISH OF INVERURIE, and forced him to retire across the Spey, thus holding all the country from Aberdeen to the Spey for the Prince (II. 344, S.M. 589).

Dec. 23rd. The two regiments of foot and two of cavalry sent to Stirling in November recalled to Edinburgh, along with the Glasgow and Paisley militia (S.M. 1746, p. 30).

---

[1] Traditionally the Prince stayed in the Buck Hotel, in High Street.

[2] A room in the Commercial Hotel is by tradition pointed out as his lodging.

[3] Drumlanrig exists as in 1745. A picture of William III., cut by claymores, preserves the tradition of the visit.

[4] Burned down in 1758, and since rebuilt. The Highlanders carried off the traditional sword of Good Sir James Douglas, which was recovered after Culloden (D.B. II. 467, 597).

[5] That these Highlanders were very half-hearted in their opposition to the Prince is evident from James Grant's narrative (III. 7), and many other contemporary sources. Cf. II. 83-85, also p. 90, *post*. Even in the regular army there were strong Jacobites. A soldier of St. Clair's regiment (1st) received 1000 lashes at Pontefract for drinking the Prince's health and saying half the regiment would join him (*Daily Advertiser*, Oct. 26).

Dec. 24-25. Marched to Hamilton, the Prince occupying Hamilton Palace.[1] Halted a day, which the Prince spent in hunting (II. 124).

Hay of Restalrig sent to Glasgow to demand a contribution of clothing and money, under pain of military execution (C.C. 62).[2]

,, 26. The Prince entered Glasgow in the afternoon[3] on foot, at the head of the clans, and occupied the Shawfield mansion in Trongate, the house of Mr. Glassford [now the site of Glassford Street] (C. C. 62, M.K. 89).

,, 27-31. Halted at Glasgow, where he kept up considerable state. The Prince reviewed his whole army on Glasgow Green,[4] and had the satisfaction to find he had lost very few men during the expedition to England (M.K. 90).[5]

Dec. 30. CARLISLE SURRENDERED.[6]

Cumberland reached Carlisle on the 21st, sent to White-haven for battering guns, opened fire on the 28th. Carlisle surrendered at discretion on the 30th (L.G. Jan. 2). *The Duke returned to London on Jan. 5th* (ib. 4-7).

---

[1] No tradition of this visit survives locally.

[2] The Jacobite party were doubly exasperated against Glasgow, which had not only not sent any body of men to join the Prince's army, but had raised a battalion for the Government service. The exactions paid in December were reimbursed by Government in 1749 by a payment of £10,000, which included the £5,500 paid to the Prince in September. A contemporary account of the Jacobite occupation of Glasgow will be found in the *Cochrane Correspondence.*

[3] It is a proof of the difficulty of fixing the exact dates of the events of this expedition that even so important an event as the entry into Glasgow is variously stated by contemporary chroniclers. Lord Elcho calls it the 27th (C.C. 142), the Lockhart chronicler the 27th (L.P. 499), Gibb and Goodwillie the 27th and 28th (II. 124, 195), but Provost Cochrane of Glasgow (C.C. 62), Lord George Murray (L.G.M. 77), Maxwell of Kirkconnell (M.K. 89), and the *London Gazette*, (L.G., Dec. 28-31), all unite on the 26th.

[4] 'It was the first general review he had made since he left the Highlands. Hitherto he had carefully concealed his weakness; but now thinking himself sure of doubling his army in a few days, he was not unwilling to let the world see with what a handful of men he had penetrated so far into England, and retired almost without any loss. It was, indeed, a very extraordinary expedition, whether we consider the boldness of the undertaking, or the conduct in the execution' (M.K. 90).

[5] 'We entered England on 8th of Nov. and left it on the 20th of Dec. without losing more than forty men' (C.J. 76, cf. L.P. 498).

[6] A list of the officers taken is printed in the *London Gazette*, January 4-7: 114 English, 274 Scots, 18 French, 406 of all ranks were captured.

1746.

Jan. 1-2   At Glasgow.

During the Prince's absence in England a considerable army had been collected, of which the headquarters were Perth and Dunblane. Though Lord Lewis Gordon had difficulty in raising the Gordons, as the Duke would not come out,[1] he collected many men from Aberdeenshire, including a regiment under Moir of Stonywood, and one under Gordon of Avochy and the Farquharsons from Deeside under Monaltrie (S.C.M. 337, 413, II. 344). Lady MacIntosh raised her clan under MacGillvray of Dunmaglass (III. 55), as her husband had joined the Government. Lady Fortrose (Seaforth), whose husband was also with Loudon, raised a few MacKenzies.[2] Lord Cromarty, with his son, Lord MacLeod, joined with a MacKenzie regiment. MacDonald of Barrisdale, young Glengarry and the elder Lochiel brought reinforcements from the west, and Glengyle some MacGregors from Perthshire. The Master of Lovat led out the clan of Fraser. Lord John Drummond, who had with him the French auxiliaries, assumed the command in chief, which had been intrusted to Lord Strathallan (L.M.N. 383 seq., etc., etc.)

„   3.   Left Glasgow in two columns, one under the Prince by Kilsyth, the other under Lord George Murray by Cumbernauld. The intention was to form a junction near Stirling with Lord John Drummond, who was marching from Perth with the army collected there (M.K. 94, L.G.M. 77). The Prince lay at Shawfield House,[3] Kilsyth (S.M. 32, II. 195 n 6).

Lord George Murray's column, consisting of six clan battalions and Lord Elcho's cavalry, halted at Cumbernauld, and marched the following day to Falkirk, whence Lochiel's regiment was sent to Alloa to escort the artillery to Stirling and subsequently to form the Prince's guard at Bannockburn (L.G.M. 77).

„   4.   The Prince marched towards Stirling, took up his

---

[1] Details of events in and about Aberdeen at this period will be found in *Bisset's Diary* and the *Stonywood Correspondence*, both printed in the SPALDING CLUB *Miscellany*, vol. I.; *The Chiefs of Grant*, vol. II. etc.

[2] They joined later (S.M. 142).

[3] The old house of Shawfield still stands, and the tradition of the Prince's visit is preserved.

Jan. 4.   headquarters at Bannockburn House[1] (Sir Hugh
                  Paterson's), and the troops occupied the villages
                  around—St. Ninians and Bannockburn (II. 195,
                  C.J. 82, etc.).

„ 5.   The Prince at Bannockburn House until the 16th
                  (II. 126).

                  During the halt at Bannockburn the Prince was joined
                  by the reinforcements that had been assembling around
                  Perth and Dunblane during his absence in England, in
                  all about 4000 men (C.J. 83, L.M.N. 383, 390, etc.).
                  While at Bannockburn the Prince was visited privately
                  by Sir John Douglas, M.P., with a private message
                  from the London Jacobites, who stated that £10,000
                  were ready for him in London.[2]

„ 6.   The town of Stirling summoned (II. 195).

                  *On Jan. 6th Hawley, who had been appointed to com-
                  mand in Scotland, reached Edinburgh; between the 2nd
                  and the 10th ten battalions of foot arrived there, and
                  Cobham's dragoons on the 15th (S.M. 32, 34).*

„ 8.   The town of Stirling capitulated (II. 196), General
                  Blakeney retiring to the castle.

„ 9-12.   At Bannockburn and Stirling (II. 129).

„ 13-14. Lord George Murray learning that the Government
                  troops were advancing from Edinburgh, marched
                  his five battalions and Elcho's and Pitsligo's horse
                  from Falkirk to Linlithgow, but on the approach
                  of General Hawley's troops returned to Falkirk,
                  and on the 14th joined the Prince at Bannockburn
                  (L.G.M. 79).

                  *On Jan. 13th Hawley's advance guard, under Huske,
                  marched from Edinburgh to Linlithgow, and the main body
                  on the 15th, Hawley following with Cobham's dragoons on
                  the 16th.[3] Huske marched to Falkirk on the 16th, where
                  he was joined by Lieut.-Colonel Campbell, with 1000 Argyle-
                  shire militia (S.M. 35).*

„ 15-16. The army drawn up in line of battle at Bannockburn
                  awaiting an attack from Hawley (L.G.M. 79).

---

[1] The old house, though altered and considerably added to, still stands.
[2] State Papers Domestic : Examination of John Murray of Broughton, August
13, 1746.
[3] Hawley's army, see additional note, p. 97.

Jan. 17.   Having been joined by all the reinforcements expected (L.G.M. 79), and not yet attacked by Hawley, the Prince with the army marched to Falkirk, leaving 1200 men under the Duke of Perth to proceed with the siege of Stirling Castle. In the evening met the enemy and defeated them at THE BATTLE OF FALKIRK.[1] The Government troops retired to Edinburgh, the Prince lodged in Falkirk in Mr. Menzies's house [2] (II. 163).

„ 18.   The Prince at Falkirk. Young Glengarry (Angus) accidentally shot (L. P. 503). Stirling Castle summoned to surrender by the Duke of Perth (II. 129).

„ 19.   The Prince returned to Bannockburn with the lowland troops ; Lord George Murray with the clans remained at Falkirk (L.G.M. 96).

„ 20-27.   The Prince at Bannockburn prosecuting the siege of Stirling Castle.[3]

„ 28.   The Prince at Bannockburn, where, learning that the Duke of Cumberland was about to join the Government army, he sent Murray of Broughton to Lord George Murray at Falkirk to prepare a plan of battle (M.K. 111).

„ 29.   The Prince at Bannockburn. Lord George Murray and the Highland chiefs at Falkirk sent a letter to the Prince, requesting him to retire to the Highlands as the army through sickness and desertion was not fit to meet the Duke of Cumberland (M.K. 111). To this course the Prince most reluctantly agreed.[4]

---

[1] Accounts of the battle are in all the contemporary narratives and journals.

[2] Traditionally, No. 121 High Street, now a shop. The title-deeds show that in 1746 it belonged to Mrs. Graham, described by Mr. Gillespie in *Round about Falkirk* as the widow of a physician, a Jacobite, and a woman of superior intelligence and manners. I have not traced Mr. Menzies. His name is not in L.P.R.

[3] The futile siege operations were under the charge of M. Mirabelle de Gordon, a French engineer, on whose ignorance and incapacity the Chevalier Johnstone pours his contempt (C.J. 89). Lord George Murray says, Mirabelle understood his business, but was so volatile he could not be depended on (L.G.M. 96), while Lord MacLeod states that he was always drunk (L.M.N. 384). Before the siege was intrusted to Mirabelle, Grant, the chief of artillery, had communicated a plan, which, though feasible, exposed the town to destruction from the castle, and was abandoned (C.J. 89).

[4] See Appendix, p. 75.

Jan. 30-31. Preparations made for the retreat (M.K. 111). On the 31st Lord George Murray retired on Bannock-burn (L.G.M. 99).

Feb. 1. The retreat begun. At a general review in the morning 'there was hardly the appearance of an army' (M.K. 114). The Church of St. Ninians blown up by accident. The troops crossed the Forth at the Fords of Frew. The Prince lodged at Drummond Castle [1] (II. 132) and the army in Dunblane, Doune, and neighbouring villages (M.K. 115).

„ 2. Part of the army marched to Perth, the clans and most of the foot to Crieff, where the Prince reviewed them and found fewer desertions than had been reported (*ib.*).

At a council of war it was resolved that the army should divide, Lord George Murray and Lord John Drummond with the Lowland regiments and the horse taking the coast road to Inverness by Montrose and Aberdeen. The Prince with the clans to go by the Highland road (L.G.M. 100, M.K. 116); Lord Ogilvy's regiment and the Farquharsons (S.C.M. 434), being near their own country, were to take a middle line by Coupar-Angus, Glen Clova, and Glen Muick to Speyside, by which means the men might visit their homes on the march.[2] This day Lord George Murray went to Perth with his column (L.G.M. 100).

The Prince lodged at Fairnton,[3] Lord John Drummond's house (II. 132).

„ 3. The Prince at Fairnton (*ib.*).

„ 4-5. The Prince went to Weem (now Castle Menzies), and halted a day (*ib.*).

The Prince's column marched by Taybridge and Tummel Bridge to Dalnacardoch. The artillery and baggage by Dunkeld and Blair Atholl (A.)

„ 6-9. The Prince went to Blair Castle [4] (S.M. 87).

On Jan. 25th Cumberland was appointed to command in Scotland (L.G. Jan. 21-25), and arrived in Edinburgh January 30th (ib. Feb. 1-4), reached Linlithgow Feb. 1,

---

[1] Drummond Castle has been rebuilt, but the rooms occupied by the Prince, though altered, still exist.

[2] Stuart's account of this march is given in the Spalding Club *Miscellany*.

[3] Now called Ferntower, the property of Lord Abercromby. The tradition of the Prince's visit has nearly died out in the neighbourhood.

[4] There is no record of the Prince's route to Blair, but he would naturally accompany his army to Tummel Bridge and take the road across the hill to the Ford on the Garry, a mile above Blair (A.).

Feb. 6-9.   *on which night the old royal palace there was burned down by*
              the soldiers' carelessness (E.E.C. Feb. 3, S.M. 48), reached
              Stirling the 2nd, where the van of his army had gone the
              day before (ib. 6). He reached Dunblane on the 4th, Crieff
              the 5th, and Perth the 6th, where he halted, sending out
              garrisons to Dunkeld and Castle Menzies, and later, under
              Sir Andrew Agnew, to Blair Castle, three battalions of foot
              to Coupar-Angus, and a regiment of dragoons to Dundee.
              The garrison of Fort William was strengthened by 300
              Argyleshire militia, and three companies of Guise's regiment
              (R.H., S.M. 81-89).

„ 10.   The barracks at Ruthven captured by Glenbucket [1]
              (S.M. 89). The Prince at Dalnacardoch, 'a public
              house on Wade's Road' (II. 134).

„ 11.   The Prince at Dalnacardoch or Dalwhinny.[2]

„ 12-14.   The Prince at Ruthven of Badenoch.[3]

„ 15.   At the house of Grant of Dalrachny.[4]

              On the 8th 4000 or 5000 Hessians,[5] under Prince
              Frederick of Hesse and Lord Crawford, arrived in Leith.
              Cumberland went to Edinburgh on the 15th, and ordered the
              Hessians to Perth and Stirling, and two regiments of
              cavalry to be stationed at Bannockburn, to prevent the
              Highlanders slipping past him to the south. He returned
              to Perth next day (S.M. 89-91).

„ 16.   The Prince went to Moy Hall,[6] the seat of the Chief of
              MacIntosh. Entertained by Lady MacIntosh (II. 134)
              (the Chief himself had joined the Government).

              On the 16th, Lord Loudon, hearing the Prince had but
              few followers with him, marched from Inverness during
              the night with a force of about 1500, intending to surprise
              and capture the Prince (S.M. 91).

---

[1] A different version of this capture, and dated the 8th, is given in C.G. II. 237.

[2] Gibb goes hopelessly wrong in his dates here.   The dates are taken from news-letters printed in C. G. vol. ii. pp. 233-236.   The distance from Dalnacardoch to Ruthven is twenty-five miles, and though there is no record of it, the probability is that the Prince spent a night at Dalwhinny (A.).

[3] There is a tradition that the Prince stayed in the old part of the present farmhouse of Ruthven, which has since been renovated and altered.

[4] The traditional halting-place was the old house of Inverlaidnan, still standing.   This date is given from inference.   He spent one night here before reaching Moy.   Gibb's *Narrative* shows that he was at Dalrachny's on part of a Sunday (II. 166).   The 16th was Sunday, on which day he must have left for Moy, where he undoubtedly was on the 16th.

[5] Dutch and Hessian troops, see additional note, p. 88.

[6] The old house was burned down early in the present century, and its site is marked by a stone near the garden.   The bed in which the Prince slept, and the bonnet he wore, are still preserved in Moy.

Feb. 16.   Having received warning of the attack, **Lady MacIntosh** at night ludicrously defeated and drove back Lord Loudon, by the stratagem of a few retainers, at the Rout of Moy (i. 149, ii. 134, 245, and most of contemporary narratives).

 ,, 17.   The Prince at Moy (ii. 135), where he collected two or three thousand men (M.K. 118).

 ,, 18.   The Prince marched to Castlehill,[1] his army entered Inverness, two miles off (ii. 137 *n*).

> *On the 18th Lord Loudon, who had command of boats, leaving a garrison in Inverness under Grant of Rothiemurchus, embarked his men and crossed the Kessack Ferry to the Black Isle* (S.M. 92).

 ,, 19.   The Prince at Culloden House,[2] where Lord George Murray joined him (L.G.M. 103).

 ,, 20.   Inverness Castle surrendered to the Prince (ii. 138 *n*, S.M. 91).

> On the retreat of the Lowland troops from Stirling by the coast road, the greater part of that force left Aberdeen on Feb. 11th (S.M. 89, S.C.M. 380), and were cantoned in the towns and villages of the north-eastern counties. Lord George Murray pushed on to Inverness, leaving garrisons at Elgin and Nairn to prevent Loudon from joining Cumberland, which he desired to do. Lord George rejoined the Prince at Culloden House on the 19th (L.G.M. 103, S.M. 92).
>
> About Feb. 21st a detachment of Berwick's [French] regiment [seems to have] landed at Peterhead (M.K. 121, S.M. 90). On the 22nd a detachment of 121 of Fitzjames's Regiment of Horse[3] arrived from France at Aberdeen, but without horses (M.K. 121, S.M. 90); the following day Aberdeen was finally evacuated (S.C.M. 384).
>
> *On the 20th Cumberland's army began the march from Perth to Aberdeen by Montrose. The van of the army reached Aberdeen on the 25th, and the Duke two days later* (S.M. 91-92).

---

[1] This may have been a house on the site of the present Castlehill house built early this century, but there is no tradition of a visit preserved.

[2] The house is still standing and the tradition and relics carefully preserved.

[3] Two of Fitzjames's transports, the *Bourbon* and the *Charité*, with 359 of all ranks, including the Count de Fitzjames, were captured by English cruisers. A list of the officers is printed in the *London Gazette*, Feb. 25-Mar. 1.

Feb. 20.   The Prince had now principally three things in view : (1) to reduce Fort Augustus and Fort William ; (2) to disperse Lord Loudon's army ; (3) to keep possession of the coast towards Aberdeen, which was the only source of obtaining supplies (M.K. 118).

Feb. 21- ⎱ The Prince in the neighbourhood of Inverness, either
Mar. 2. ⎰ at Castlehill or Culloden.[1]

Mar. 3-10. The Prince went to Inverness and lodged in the house of the Dowager Lady MacIntosh [2] until the 10th (II. 139).

„ 11 20. The Prince went to Elgin, where he became very ill.[3] He visited Gordon Castle before his return to Inverness (II. 142, S.M. 137).

At Elgin John Murray of Broughton became very ill, and did not again see the Prince. He was succeeded as Secretary by John Hay of Restalrig.[4]

---

[1] The confusion of this part of Gibb's Journal and the want of other evidence makes it impossible to fix the Prince's exact location. Lord George Murray says he visited the Prince at Culloden the day before Inverness surrendered. Gibb represents him as lodging several days at Castlehill and several at Culloden, but his dates between January 31 and March 3 are avowedly untrustworthy (II. 138 *n*).

[2] Anna Duff of Drumuir, widow of Lachlan, 20th of MacIntosh. There were then two dowagers. The house was on the west side of Church Street, nearly opposite St. John's Episcopal Church. It was taken down in 1843. Cumberland occupied the same rooms after Culloden.

[3] There is little contemporary record of the Prince's visit to Elgin. The newspapers of the day mention his visit and his illness (S.M. 137). Local tradition says he lodged in Thunderton House as the guest of Mrs. Anderson of Arradoul, and that he daily, when able, visited Gordon Castle. The Duke of Gordon had left the Castle, ' on foot, and in the most secret manner he could,' and joined Cumberland at Aberdeen two days before the Prince's arrival (S.M. 138). A letter from Colonel Warren to the Prince's father, written from Paris, May 9, 1746, now at Windsor, mentions his illness, and that ' a timely bleeding hindered the cold turning into a fluxion *de poitrine*, and caused a joy in every heart not to be described.' The letter is printed in B.H., Stuart Papers, App. xxviii. Thunderton House is in Batchen Lane, off High Street. It was formerly a residence of the Earls of Moray. Though some of it has been taken down, a large part of the old house still stands ; part is now used as a restaurant. There is no 'Prince Charles's room' in Gordon Castle, and no tradition of his visit.

[4] State Papers : Examination of John Murray, . . . 1746. Hay was much blamed for his mismanagement of the commissariat in the critical days before Culloden. Lord George Murray compares him very unfavourably with John Murray, ' who had always been extremely active in whatsoever regarded the providing for the army' (I. 260). It is stated that the army starved while there was abundance of stores at Inverness (I. 86, 260; M.K. 141, 142; L.G.M. 122, J.M.B., State Papers, etc.).

Mar. 11-20. Brigadier Stapleton, with some of the French troops, and Lochiel and Keppoch, were sent to attack Fort Augustus and Fort William. The siege of Fort Augustus began on March 3rd, and the fort surrendered on the 5th (M.K. 119). The same day the Highlanders attacked Fort William, and on the 7th the French troops with artillery arrived (S.M. 139). Operations were begun by Grant the engineer, who was wounded early in the siege, and Mirabelle had to be employed 'and succeeded no better at Fort William than he had done at Stirling'[1] (M.K. 121). On the 31st the garrison made a sally, and destroyed the besiegers' batteries and captured some of their guns. The siege was abandoned on April 4th, and the troops returned to Inverness (I. 356; II. 270; S.M. 140, 183).

After the capture of Inverness Lord Cromarty was despatched with Glengarry, Clanranald, Appin, Glengyle, MacKinnon, and some MacKenzies in pursuit, but having no boats was obliged to go round by the head of the firth, and upon his approach Loudon retired across the Dornoch Firth to Dornoch. When Cromarty attempted to pursue him by land he recrossed the firth into Ross-shire, and about the 2nd March Cromarty returned to Tain, upon which Loudon again crossed to Dornoch. Cromarty was then superseded in command by the Duke of Perth, and returned to Inverness. Finding land operations useless, a large number of boats were collected at Findhorn by Moir of Stonywood, and brought to Tain during a fog, which concealed them from the English cruisers. On March 20th Perth's force crossed into Sutherland by sea, and completely dispersed Loudon's force (I. 355, 358, L.G.M. 103, 111, M.K. 128, S.M. 91, 144, L.M.N. 396, A.C., etc.). Perth returned to Inverness, and joined Drummond on the Spey (M.K. 138).

Lord Loudon, with President Forbes and MacLeod of MacLeod, retired to Skye, and Lord Reay to his own country (II. 270, S.M. 144).

March 15th. Lord George Murray made a rapid march into Perthshire with his Atholl battalion, and was joined at Ruthven by Cluny MacPherson, who had remained in Badenoch to guard the passes there (I. 356). On the early morning of the 17th he simultaneously surprised thirty posts of the government and took them all. On

---

[1] Lord George Murray says: 'Brigadier Stapleton and I had no hopes of success by what had happened at Stirling, which was not so strong' (L.G.M. 106). A Journal of the siege by an English officer is printed in S.M. 140, 181.

Mar. 11-20.   the same day he attacked Blair Castle, then defended by
Sir Andrew Agnew.[1] While blockading it he gathered
a reinforcement of about 500 men from his brother's
country. By March 27th Lord Crawford, preceded by
the Prince of Hesse and followed by St. George's
Dragoons, had advanced from Perth to Dunkeld (A.), and
on April 2nd the siege was abandoned. Lord George returned to Inverness, his infantry marched to Elchies on
the Spey, while Cluny remained to guard the passes of
Badenoch (I. 356, II. 91, L.G.M. 107-110, S.M. 143-144,
L.G. Mar. 29-Apr. 1).

„ 21-31. The Prince at Inverness (II. 144).

Lord John Drummond was intrusted with the defence of the Spey. He fixed his headquarters at Gordon
Castle, with his cavalry at Cullen and Strathbogie.
His infantry occupied Strathbogie, Keith, Fochabers,
Elgin, and neighbouring places; Kilmarnock's cavalry
was reformed as infantry, and the horses given to Fitzjames's squadron (M.K. 122, 123).

*March 12th. General Bland was sent with a strong force to
Inverurie and Old Meldrum, and on the 16th, strengthened by
four battalions under Mordaunt, marched to Strathbogie
on the 17th, and nearly surprised Roy Stewart* (S.M. 145).

On March 17th Roy Stewart and the forces at Strathbogie retired to Keith and thence to Fochabers (M.K. 123).
On the 20th Major Glascoe,[2] with a small miscellaneous
force, marched by night to Keith, which had been occupied
by a party of Campbell's Argyleshire militia and Kingston's horse, and in the early morning surprised and
captured nearly the whole garrison at the SKIRMISH OF
KEITH (II. 212, M.K. 127, etc.).

*On the 26th the first line of six battalions and two cavalry
regiments were at Strathbogie, under Lord Albemarle and
Bland; reserve of three battalions and four guns under
Mordaunt at Old Meldrum; and the remainder—six battalions and one cavalry regiment—at Aberdeen* (S.M. 145).

On March 25th the *Hazard* sloop (which had been fitted
out by the Prince and renamed the *Prince Charles*),
returning from France with money and stores, was pursued by four English cruisers in the Pentland Firth,
and forced to run ashore at Tongue. Lord Reay,

---

[1] A detailed narrative of the siege by Melville of Strathkinness, an officer in
Sempill's (25th) is printed in S.M. 1808, pp. 330, 410.

[2] Nicholas Glascoe was a native of France, a lieutenant in Dillon's regiment.
He had raised the battery against the *Hazard*. He was captured and tried, but
escaped on account of his French commission (S.M. 527, 529).

Mar.-April.   learning of its arrival, captured 156 of all ranks[1] and
£12,000.   Lord Cromarty and his son, Lord MacLeod,
with whom were Barrisdale, Glengyle, and MacKinnon
(II. 275), were sent with a force of 1500 men to attempt
the recovery of the treasure, and to raise men and money
for the Prince in Sutherland and Caithness.   The commanders were surprised and made prisoners at Dunrobin
Castle by the retainers of Lords Sutherland and Reay on
April 15th (I. 358 ; II. 271 ; M.K. 135 ; L.G.M. 113 ; also
Sir William Fraser's *Sutherland Book*, I. 418-20).

April 1-13.   The Prince at Inverness (II. 147).

*Cumberland left Aberdeen on 8th April, concentrated his
army at Cullen on 11th, being there joined by Albemarle;
crossed the Spey without loss on the 12th, reached Elgin
the 13th, and encamped at Alves; Nairn the 14th, and
halted the 15th,* CUMBERLAND'S BIRTHDAY (S.M. 184).

As Cumberland advanced, Perth and Drummond retired before him by Forres and Nairn to Culloden,
which they reached on the 14th (S.C.M. 343).

„ 14.   The Prince marched to Culloden House (I. 66.)

„ 15.   At Culloden.[2] Marched by night towards Nairn to
surprise Cumberland, but owing to delays on the
march and the advent of daylight was obliged to
abandon the attack[3] (I. 254, 360, etc.) when within
three miles of Nairn (H. H. 223 *n.*).

„ 16   Marched back in the morning to Drummossie or
Culloden Muir, where the Prince, learning that
Cumberland was close at hand, determined to fight,
against the judgment of Lord George Murray and
the Highland chiefs[4] (I. 86, L.G.M. 123).   At 1
o'clock fighting began, and in twenty-five minutes
(M.S.L. 62, 65) the Prince was defeated at the
BATTLE OF CULLODEN.[5]

[1] A list of the officers captured is printed in the *London Gazette*, Apr. 12-15.

[2] An account of the Prince visiting Kilravock on the 15th, dining there, and
returning to Culloden is given in Mr. Bain's *Nairnshire*, 1893, p. 352.

[3] Mr. Andrew Lang in an article in *Bibliographica*, III. 411, 1896, mentions that
he has seen, in the Stuart Papers at Windsor, a letter of 1759, from the Prince to
his father stating that the night attack might have succeeded after all, as Clanranald had come upon Cumberland's outposts and found them unprepared.

[4] 'Our time was come. We were at variance within ourselves: Irish intriguers and
French politics were too predominant in our councils.'—Sir Robert Strange (M.S.L.
I. 60).   'We were obliged to be undone for their ease.'—Letter of Lord George
Murray (H.H. 368); but cf. the Prince's statement to MacEachain, App. p. 80.

[5] The most graphic account of the night march and the battle is given by Sir
Robert Strange (M.S.L. I. 57).   The Government account with list of prisoners,
etc., is printed in L.G. April 26.

April 16.   The remains of the army retired to Corrybrough;
17th to Balnaspiech by Aviemore; 18th to Ruthven,
(S.C.M. 343). On or before the 20th the army at Ruthven received a message from the Prince to seek their
own safety, and the army dispersed.[1]

On May 8th at Muirlaggan (Loch Arkaig) an endeavour
was made to organise another rising, but the attempt
proved abortive (I. 88, H.H. 384).

*Between the 23rd and 30th April Cumberland was joined
by 4 battalions from England. Cobham's and Lord Mark
Kerr's Dragoons left Inverness for the East Coast. Lord
Loudon, with MacLeod and Sir Alexander MacDonald,
came from Skye to Lochaber with 1700 men, and joined
General Campbell, who brought 800 Argyleshire Militia, to
clear Lochaber. Different bodies of militia were sent to
different districts in the Highlands* (S.M. 237).

*On May 19th, Brigadier Mordaunt, with 3 battalions,
left for Perth to relieve the Hessians, who were sent back
viâ Leith to Holland. On 22nd and 23rd, the Duke, with
an army composed of Kingston's Horse and 11 battalions of
foot, marched to Fort-Augustus; and on 24th, a battalion
left for Aberdeen, leaving 4 battalions at Inverness.
Parties were sent to scour Badenoch and Lochaber, and
'all round the Highlands,' 'wherever these came, they left
nothing that belonged to the rebels.' On the 30th, Cumberland paid a flying visit to Fort-William* (S.M. 240,284-286).

---

[1] There is much confusion about the message from the Prince to the army.
From Gortleg the A.D.C. Alexr. MacLeod wrote to Cluny stating there was
to be a review of the clans the following day at Fort Augustus, and requesting him
to join there. That the chiefs of the army had no common understanding, and
that this order was incomprehensible to Lord George Murray is shown by his com-
ments indorsed on it, which are printed along with MacLeod's letter in A.C. 220.
Ker of Graden states that the army stayed at Ruthven some days awaiting an
answer which did not come when expected, and in consequence they dispersed
(I.363). Kirkconnell says young Sheridan was sent to the leaders immediately after
the battle to tell them to shift for themselves (M.K. 158). The Chevalier Johnstone—not a very reliable authority—says that MacLeod was sent by Lord George
to the Prince, and returned on the 20th with the laconic answer, 'Let every one
seek the means of escape as well as he can' (C.J. 167), which, if true, means that
the A.D.C. must have gone from Stratherrick to Ruthven (about 25 miles) with
the original letter, gone back at once with Lord George's message, by which
time the Prince had gone to Loch Arkaig, and again returned to Ruthven on the
20th—a very unlikely circumstance. Lumisden, one of his secretaries quoted
by Home (H.H. 240), states that the day following the battle the Prince sent a
message to Ruthven thanking his friends for their bravery and devotion, and
desiring them to do what they thought best for their own preservation.

April 16.   After the battle of Culloden the Prince crossed the river Nairn at the ford of Falie, where he dismissed his cavalry escort (I. 190). Accompanied by Lord Elcho, Sheridan, Alexander MacLeod, O'Sullivan, Peter MacDermit (*ib.*), O'Neil (I. 367), and guided by Edward Burke, he rode by Tordarroch, Aberarder, and Faroline to Gortleg,[1] where he met Lord Lovat. Rode on by Fort Augustus (I. 68).[2]

„ 17.   Arrived in early morning at Invergarry Castle,[3] and rested there or at Droynachan until 3 in the afternoon. The Prince, O'Sullivan, Allan MacDonald (a priest), and Burke (I. 191, 321) rode on by Loch Arkaig to Glenpean, and there spent the night in the house of Donald Cameron (I. 191).[4]

„ 18.   Remained at Glenpean awaiting intelligence until 5 P.M., when he started on foot across the hills for Glen Morar (I. 69).

„ 19.   Arrived in the braes of Morar, utterly tired out, and was entertained by Angus MacEachine, Borradale's son-in-law, in 'a small sheal house near a wood' (I. 191, 322, N.M'E. 324).[5]

---

[1] Now called Gortleck or Gorthlick. The house still stands.

[2] The moon was near her first quarter, and set about 2 A.M.

[3] Most narratives represent the Prince as having spent a night at Invergarry Castle, while Glenaladale states that he spent the night at Droynachan's house (I. 321 and L.P. 540). I believe that all the stories refer to the same event. The Prince remained in the neighbourhood from 2 A.M. till 3 P.M. Droynachan is within a mile of Invergarry, which was deserted, and the party possibly visited both. Burke's version of the story is here followed, as he was the actual companion of the Prince. The other stories are mere hearsay. Invergarry Castle was shortly afterwards burned.

[4] Until 1893 a cottage stood at Kinloch Arkaig, at the mouth of Glen Pean, in which, tradition firmly held, the Prince had found shelter. There can be no doubt that if he occupied it, it must have been on this occasion, while he was awaiting news of his army, as this is the only time that there is any record of his visiting the head of Loch Arkaig. Unfortunately about three years ago the cottage took fire and was burned down, and with it the bed in which the Prince slept. A photograph by a lady has been preserved, of which Mr. Andrew Lang showed me a copy. It is an ordinary Highland cottage, with a heather-thatched roof.

[5] Burke calls the halting-place Mewboll [Meoble] (I. 191), and Alexander MacDonald, Oban. These are neighbouring glens in the district of Morar, and the shelter was likely in a wood somewhere between them. Chambers makes them stay the first night at Meoble and the second at Oban; Ewald and Jesse both follow Chambers. They appear to have been misled by the two narratives,

April 20. At night walked to Borradale by Glenbeasdale, 'which is a pendicle belonging to the ffarm of Borradil' (III. 376).

„ 21. Met Donald MacLeod, tenant of Gualtergill,[1] at Borradale, who had been sent as a guide by Æneas MacDonald, Kinlochmoidart's brother (I. 161).

> The Prince's object was to go to Sir Alexander MacDonald or MacLeod of MacLeod for protection, but Donald refused to take him (I. 162), and arranged instead to guide him to the Hebrides, in hopes of getting a vessel thence to France, or, failing that, to Orkney (I. 69).

„ 22–25. Remained in the neighbourhood of Borradale while Donald MacLeod procured a boat and a crew (I. 163).
From Borradale the Prince wrote a formal farewell letter to the chiefs[2] (I. 103, 368).

„ 26. The Prince sailed from Borradale, Lochnanuagh, at night,[3] accompanied by O'Sullivan, O'Neil, Allan MacDonald, Donald MacLeod, and Edward Burke, and by seven boatmen (I. 163).[4]

---

and there is no authority for the statement that the Prince went first to Meoble and then turned back to Oban.

[1] Gualtergill is on Loch Dunvegan in Skye.

[2] This letter, preserved in the Stuart Papers at Windsor, is printed in the text of Browne's *History* (B.H. III. 263). It was left with John Hay to be sent to Sheridan for delivery, but I have not been able to find any evidence that it ever reached those to whom it was addressed. In the letter he advises the chiefs to defend themselves till the French assisted them, and to take any measures they considered best. He himself would go to France, either to obtain active assistance, or at least to procure through the French court better terms for his followers. His return to France would thwart the traditional French policy, which was not to restore James, but to keep up a continual civil war in Britain. He finally requests them to conceal his departure as long as possible.

Home states (H.H. 241) that Lord George Murray sent a message by Hay of Restalrig to the Prince at Borradale, imploring him not to leave Scotland. Considering the terms that they were on, and the bitter complaints Lord George had made of Hay on the 17th (see p. 80, *post*), the story is not probable. Murray of Broughton states that such a message from Lochiel and himself was sent by Dr. Cameron, who found Hay in charge, and that Hay denied him access to the Prince, so Cameron was obliged to return without delivering his message.

[3] It was two nights after the full moon, which rose that night about half-past eleven and set about sunrise.

[4] Alexander MacDonald gives this date as the 24th (I. 322), Walkinshaw and Burton give the 28th (I. 69), while O'Neil gives a confused account (I. 369) that is manifestly inaccurate. Donald MacLeod's dates are here followed; he was an actor in the drama, and a man of great intelligence (I. 271).

April 27-29. Driven by storm to Rossinish, in Benbecula,[1] in the
            morning, remained two days in a deserted hut: visited
            by Clanranald (I. 323). Determined to make for
            Stornoway, they set sail on evening of 29th (I. 166).

„   30.   Arrived at Scalpa or Glass Island[2] in early morning,
            where the Prince was entertained by Donald Camp-
            bell[3] in his farmhouse (ib.).

---

[1] The traditional place of landing and of departure to Harris is Barrà na Luinge
(*Ord. Sur.* Lingay), the only anchorage on the coast.   Near the landing-place
there are ruins of a store-house which may have formed the Prince's shelter.   A
small loch in Rossinish is locally called Loch-na-arm, because, the story goes,
the Prince's party on their return from Stornoway threw their arms into it.
My informant, Mr. John MacDonald, shepherd in Benbecula, lately found an
old dirk there.   The handle is of wood unknown in the island.   The blade,
which is five inches long, bears the initials K. K. S.   The names of the party
are given in I. 163, but none correspond to these letters.

[2] I am informed by Mrs. Flora MacLeod, a great-granddaughter of Donald
Campbell, and still resident in Scalpa, that the landing-place of the Prince was
Ard-na-hadhadh.   At that time Donald Campbell was the only tenant on the island.
His farmhouse was taken down about twenty-four years ago, and a larger house
built on the same site.   The chair the Prince traditionally used is still preserved,
or was so till quite lately, in the village of Kyles.   Mrs. MacLeod relates a
traditional anecdote that one evening the Prince, when strolling near Ard-an-
Asaig, observed one of his host's cows stuck fast in a bog : alone and unassisted
he rescued the animal, which was afterwards sold for £2, 10s., then an unheard-
of price in Harris.

[3] Donald Campbell was Baleshair's brother-in-law (II. 100).   There is
a pleasant story about his fidelity in Buchanan's *Travels in the Western
Hebrides* (1793): 'It was well known that this gentleman was strictly loyal
and well attached to the reigning Family, yet the enormous sum of thirty
thousand pounds could not bribe him to act the infamous part required.
The master of a noted family, a very bulky man, who is now alive, and resides
in an island in that country, with the clergyman at their head, landed before
day, with a boat full of armed men, on the Isle of Glass, with a determined
resolution to seize the Chevalier, and secure the bribe offered by Government.
Mr. Campbell scorned the bribe, and expostulated much against the infamous
attempt ; he also pointed out the danger of making the experiment on so many
formidable and desperate gentlemen who would chop the heads off the whole of
them before they sheathed their swords.   But when he found that they still
persisted in spite of reason, he assured them, that he himself would fall in his
cause, rather than give up the man that intrusted him with his life, or entail
shame on his posterity.   With that view he despatched his son to give them
intelligence of their danger.   The Chevalier and his party were forewarned and
armed before that gentleman arrived, and were ready to give the assailants a hot
reception, had they approached ; but they sneaked off from the island, ashamed,
and disappointed at the loss of the money, which they already had devoured in
their thoughts, and divided to every man in his due proportion.'
The clergyman was Aulay Macaulay, minister of Harris, the great-grandfather

May 1.   Donald MacLeod despatched to Stornoway to try to hire a vessel for the Orkneys. The Prince remained at Scalpa (I. 166).

„ 2–3.   The Prince at Scalpa (*ib.*).

         On May 3rd two French ships landed 40,000 louis d'ors at Borradale in spite of the attacks of H.M.S. *Greyhound* and the sloops *Baltimore* and *Terror*. The treasure was conveyed to Loch Arkaig to the care of Murray of Broughton (III. 383, S.M. 238).

„ 4.   Hearing that Donald had succeeded in hiring a brig, the Prince, attended by O'Sullivan, O'Neil and a guide, landed in Harris, and walked across country towards Stornoway (I. 167).[1]

„ 5.   Arrived in the morning at Kildun House in Arnish (within two miles of Stornoway) and there entertained by Mrs. Mackenzie. The inhabitants of Stornoway, on hearing who the visitor was, refused to let him enter the town or have the vessel, nor would they let him have a pilot for Seaforth's country (Ross-shire), where the Prince desired to go (I. 169, 191, 325, 369).

„ 6.   Left Arnish in the morning for Scalpa, but sighting some ships of war (I. 192, 325) were obliged to put in to the uninhabited island Euirn or Iffurt (*Ord. Sur.* Iubhard), where they remained four days and nights in ' a low pityful hut,' over which they had to spread the boat-sail to keep out the rain (I. 172).

„ 7–9.   At Euirn (*ib.*)

„ 10.   Sailed for Scalpa, but found that Donald Campbell had left the island, being obliged to go into hiding for the hospitality he had shown the Prince a week before. Went south; pursued by a man-of-war (Capt.

---

of Lord Macaulay. It was he who warned the Stornoway people of the Prince's arrival in the Lewis (I. 168). His son John, minister of South Uist, who had sent him word of the Prince's coming, was Lord Macaulay's grandfather, and is probably the ' devil of a minister who did us a' the mischief in his power '(I. 204). Cf. *Life of Macaulay*, chap. I. ; N.M'E. 325.

[1] Local tradition gives the route marked on the accompanying map. The party sailed to nearly the top of Loch Seaforth, and thence walked by night (losing their way) through the boggy country at the head of the many lochs, to Arnish. There was no moonlight until half-past two, shortly before daybreak, and about an hour and a half before sunrise. Kildun is now a gamekeeper's lodge, near Arnish Point.

May 10.   Ferguson) but rowed to shallow water near Rodil
               Point (I. 193) and escaped. Went along the coast
               towards Benbecula, escaping another ship at Loch
               Maddy and spent the night at sea (I. 173).

„   11.   Landed on an island in Lochwiskaway (*Ord. Sur.* Us-
               kavagh) and put up at 'a poor grass keepers bothy
               or hut' (I. 70, 173, 193).[1]

„   12–13.   At Loch Uskavagh 'about three nights' (I. 194).

„; 14.   Walked to Coradale in South Uist.[2]   Macleod was
               sent to the mainland[3] to endeavour to get some
               money for the Prince from Murray of Broughton,
               who was at Loch Arkaig, with Lochiel and others,
               and returned unsuccessful after eighteen days'
               absence (I. 174, 194, 370).

               H.M. Ships 'Greyhound,' 'Baltimore,' *and* 'Terror,'
               having repaired damages, were joined by the 'Raven' *sloop*
               on the 4th.   *H.M. Ships* 'Scarborough,' *and* 'Glasgow,'
               and the sloops 'Trial' *and* 'Happy Janet' *on the 13th,*
               and H.M.S. 'Furnace' (*Capt. Ferguson*) *on the 17th.*
               The squadron scoured the coasts (S.M. 239).

„   15–June 5. At Coradale in a forester's cottage[4] (I. 326). Here
               the Prince remained for twenty-two days (I. 370)

---

[1] Alexander MacDonald says he landed at Rairnish, which is the northern
point of the peninsula of Rossinish on the 8th (I. 325); but Donald MacLeod's
story, corroborated by Burke's, both of whom were with the Prince, seems to me
preferable, and it entirely fits in with the subsequent dates given by the later
actors in the drama.   A leaf of Donald MacLeod's narrative is unfortunately lost
here and we are obliged to fall back on Burke and O'Neil.

The dates and itinerary in South Uist are pieced together thus: Donald
MacLeod is followed and his dates accepted up to May 11th, where a portion of
his journal is mutilated.   Burke is then followed to the 14th, and then O'Neil
till June 5th.   Then Donald again takes up the story on what must have been the
6th, for it is evident that on page 268 Bishop Forbes makes a slip in his inter-
polation.   The date June 14th (I. 268) is manifestly wrong.   On the 14th they
were sailing south, and the trip to Ouia took place before that.   No more dates
are given till Flora MacDonald takes up the tale, but by following the narrative
from day to day, first by Donald MacLeod, then by Burke, and lastly by Neil
MacEachain, the dates are filled exactly up to the time of sailing to Skye.

[2] Alex. MacDonald (I. 326) says the 10th, but this is obviously wrong.   Burton
and Walkinshaw (I. 70) give the date the 14th, which also coincides with Donald
MacLeod and Edward Burke.

[3] O'Neil says that Donald MacLeod was sent from Wiskaway, but he himself
says (I. 174) he rejoined the Prince at Coradale where he had left him.

[4] A small cave in the face of a rock in the north side of a little glen near the
beach at Coradale is the traditional hiding-place of the Prince, but there is no
mention of a cave in the contemporary accounts, which indeed almost exclude

June 5.   in comparative comfort and safety; he was visited by his friends and enjoyed shooting, at which he was very expert (I. 327).[1] Learning that troops had landed in the Long Island and were hemming him in, he was obliged to move (I. 328, etc.)

„   6.   Sailed to Island Ouia (*Ord. Sur.* Wiay) (I. 268).

„   7-9. Remained at Ouia where they heard the troops were following them (I. 370).

„ 10-12. The Prince and O'Neil went to Rossinish by land, and remained three days, until they learned that the boats of the militia were patrolling the place. Donald Macleod and O'Sullivan, hearing of this, came in a boat, brought them away and steered for Coradale (I. 268).

„ 13. Forced by storm to put in at Uishness Point, they spent the night at Aikersideallach (*Ord. Sur.* Acarseid Fhalaich[2]) in the cleft of a rock (I. 195, 268).

„ 14. The enemy being within two miles of them they sailed to Ciliestiella (*Ord. Sur.* Kyle Stuley) (I. 268).

      Before the middle of June[3] General Campbell, who had gone in pursuit to the remote Western Isles (St. Kilda), had returned to Barra and South Uist (S.M. 339).

„ 15-20. Sailed for Loch Boisdale in hopes of getting assistance from MacDonald of Boisdale, but found that he had been made prisoner (I. 269). Seeing fifteen sail, and a number of the enemy being on land in the neighbourhood, they concealed themselves in a creek till night, when they entered Loch Boisdale and took shelter in an old tower 'in the mouth of the island' [traditionally Calvay], the Prince taking to the mountains until night. They skulked up and down the loch, sleeping in the open fields at night with only the boat sails for shelter (I. 196)

---

the probability of such a refuge being required (I. 74). MacEachain states that while acting as guide he left the Prince 'under a rock' while he went forward to see there were no strangers near the house (N. M'E. 334), and this may have given rise to the tradition.

[1] Alexander MacDonald gives the 10th as the date of a visit from a number of gentlemen, and of a notable carouse. This is an impossible date. It is probable that, as frequently occurs in these narratives, he was a week wrong in his reckoning, and the visit may have taken place on 3rd June, about which time Boisdale came to warn the Prince to shift his quarters (N. M'E. 331).

[2] 'The anchorage of concealment.'

[3] Misprinted 'July' in S.M., which the context shows is wrong.

June 20.   and remained in the neighbourhood for some days,[1] when Captain Carolina Scott landed within a mile of them (i. 269, 370).

                 Donald MacLeod, who here parted from the Prince, was taken prisoner a fortnight later (i. 178).

,, 21.   The Prince accompanied by O'Neil and guided by Neil MacEachain,[2] crossed the mountains and came to a hut, near Ormaclett,[3] at midnight,[4] where they met Flora MacDonald, and asked her assistance to convey the Prince to Skye, which she agreed to do. Flora left for Benbecula to make arrrangements. The Prince and his companions went to a hill three miles from Coradale (i. 196, 296, 371, N.M'E. 335).

,, 22.   MacEachain was sent to get Flora's answer, and the Prince spent the night at the same place, under a rock (N. M'E. 335). This night both MacEachain and Flora were detained by the militia guard at the ford (ib. 336).

,, 23.   MacEachain returning, guided the Prince at night to Wiay, crossing the loch in a country boat, as the fords were guarded.

,, 24.   They rowed on in the early morning to Benbecula, forded an arm of the sea, finding temporary shelter in a hut, and late at night reached Rossinish, spending the night in the house of Clanranald's booman [principal tenant] (ib. 338).

,, 25.   O'Neil was sent on to meet Flora at Nunton. The Prince and MacEachain fled from the cottage to avoid the militia, and spent the day in the open air in pouring rain, sheltered by a rock. When the militia had gone, the Prince returned and spent the night in the booman's house (ib.).

,, 26.   Awaited O'Neil and Flora in the same place (ib.)

---

[1] It could only have been six days, for each of which Burke accounts.

[2] Cf. additional note, p. 98.

[3] Ormaclett was the former residence of Clanranald in South Uist, but the house was burned down the day that Clanranald fell at Sheriffmuir, and has not been rebuilt. In 1746 Clanranald resided in Benbecula. The name of his house, Ballinnagallioch (Baile-nan-cailliach), now called Nunton, should have been translated the Carlines' (i.e. Nuns') house, not the Carl's house as at i. 326 n. Ormaclett was about three miles from Milton, Flora MacDonald's home. Chambers, Jesse, and Ewald confuse Ormaclett with Nunton.

[4] It was the night of the full moon.

June 26.   . Flora suggested that the Prince should take refuge
              with Baleshair in North Uist, instead of crossing to
              Skye, but Baleshair was obliged to decline for clan
              reasons (I. 327, 372).

„   27.   Joined by Lady Clanranald and her daughter,[1] by
              Flora MacDonald, her brother Milton, and O'Neil
              (N. M'E. 340). During supper (I. 297), learning that
              General Campbell, Capt. Scott, and Capt. Ferguson
              were closing them in with a large force (I. 372),

„   28.   The party took boat, crossed Loch Uskevagh,[2] and
              finished supper at 5 A.M. At 8 Lady Clanranald
              was summoned to Nunton to attend General Camp-
              bell (N. M'E. 340).

              Clanranald and Lady Clanranald were both taken
              prisoner shortly afterwards (I. 146, S.M. 341).

              The Prince here parted from O'Neil, who tried to re-
              join him in Skye, but finding him gone, he fled to North
              Uist, where he was taken prisoner (I. 373).

              In the evening the Prince dressed in female
              clothing as 'Betty Burke, was joined by Flora
              MacDonald, and sailed for Skye[3] (I. 298, 329).

              The party consisted of the Prince, Flora MacDonald,
              Neil MacEachain, and four boatmen (III. 22).

„   29.   Arrived off the point of Waternish in Skye, but found
              the place occupied by troops, who fired on them;
              they rowed off and rested in concealment in a

---

[1] Miss 'Peggy Clanranald' was living at Ormaclett as late as 1825 (C.F.M. 329).

[2] Flora MacDonald in her evidence before the Privy Council says, 'they sat up
all night at a shieling called Closchinisch. . . . continued there till about 9 at
night, . . . when they embarked' (State Papers, July 12, 1746). I have failed
in identifying Closchinisch, which is not known locally, but which the context
shows was on the south side of Loch Uskavagh.

[3] A tradition exists, for which there is, however, no contemporary authority,
that on starting for Skye the wind and tide were so contrary that the party
sailed up the coast to Airdmaddy, and landed there for a short time, well
out of the reach of men-of-war, to wait till the tide should slacken. They
rested and dried themselves in the cottage of Eobhan MacPherson, a crofter
and fisherman. A man named MacDonald, who had been at Culloden, coming
into the cottage recognised the Prince in the 'Ban Eirionnach mhor' (big
Irishwoman), but did not betray him. Next day he informed his host
who the visitor was, and at once a contest arose among MacPherson's three
daughters, girls in their teens, as to who should possess the stool on which the
Prince had sat. In the contest the youngest daughter lost two of her teeth.
The stool was awarded to her as having fought so valiantly and suffered so much
in the Prince's cause. (*Communicated by Mr. Alexander Carmichael, in whose
possession the stool and several other relics of Flora MacDonald still exist.*)

June 29. creek; then rowed on to Kilbride in Troternish where they landed near Mougstot [Monkstat] House.[1] Flora went to Lady Margaret MacDonald[2] at Monkstat, who sent her factor, MacDonald of Kingsburgh, to the Prince with refreshment. The Prince walked with him to Kingsburgh House,[3] where he spent the night (I. 301).

Kingsburgh was taken prisoner a few days later (I. 126).

„ 30. Late in the day started with a guide (a little boy M'Queen, II. 21) for Portree and changed his female clothes in a wood for a Highland dress (I. 76, 302). He walked to Portree with MacEachain and M'Queen by byways, while Flora rode near him on the main road. Met by Donald Roy MacDonald, who had made arrangements for conveying him to Raasa (II. 20). Spent two hours in a public-house at Portree[4] (I. 130, 302, II. 22).

July 1. Started in the early morning, by boat, from Portree (traditionally from Sgeir Mhor), for Raasa Island, conducted by Murdoch MacLeod of Raasa and Malcolm MacLeod, and spent this and the following day at Glam, in Raasa. John MacLeod, younger of Raasa, was also in the boat (I. 131, 302).

At Portree Flora MacDonald parted from the Prince and was taken prisoner eight or ten days after (I. 303).

„ 2. The Prince fearing that Raasa was too small an island for concealment, left Raasa in the evening in a boat, attended by John MacLeod, Murdoch MacLeod his brother, Malcolm MacLeod, and two boatmen, and returned to Skye, landing at night at Nicolson's Rock, near Scorobreck, and spent the night in a cow-byre[5] (I. 133).

---

[1] The traditional landing-place is named Alt a Chuain, on the beach to the north of Kilbride.

[2] It is interesting, almost ludicrous, to read the explanation of Sir Alexander and Lady Margaret to the Lord President (C.P. 290, 291).

[3] Kingsburgh House has entirely disappeared. A few trees only mark the site.

[4] A room in the older part of the Royal Hotel, Portree, is traditionally shown as the Prince's resting-place.

[5] A cave about four miles to the north of Portree is figured on the Ordnance Survey as 'Prince Charles's Cave.' There is no authority for it whatever. The Prince, we are told, landed at Nicolson's Rock (Creag Mhicneucail, a long scaur running along the north side of Portree harbour; and the traditional, and indeed the only possible, landing-place is Lag na Bachagh (the

July 3. Remained in the byre until evening,[1] when, parting from the brothers and the boatmen, the Prince walked all night,[2] attended by Malcolm MacLeod, towards Strath, MacKinnon's country, the Prince passing as Lewie Caw, MacLeod's servant (I. 134).

,, 4. Early morning arrived at Ellagol (*Ord. Sur.* Elgol), at the house of John MacKinnon,[3] MacLeod's brother-in-law, and were hospitably entertained. Here the Prince met the old Chief of MacKinnon, who took the management of the expedition into his own hands, and at night[4] he and John MacKinnon and four boatmen embarked with the Prince in a boat for the mainland (I. 139, 152, 277; II. 31, 81, 186).

Malcolm MacLeod, who left the Prince here, was made prisoner a few days later (I. 144).

,, 5–7. Arrived at little Mallack[5] (*Ord. Sur.* Mallaig), on Loch Nevis, in the early morning of the 5th, where they landed, and lay three nights in the open air (II. 251).

,, 8. The Chief having gone to seek a better refuge, the Prince and John MacKinnon rowed up Loch Nevis along the coast, when they were chased by some militia; but, outdistancing them, the Prince jumped ashore and climbed a hill,[6] where he slept for three

hollow of the byre) about two miles south of the cave. The fact that he spent the night in the byre above this hollow precludes the possibility of the cave being used as the Prince's hiding-place. These names are not on the *Ord. Sur.*

[1] It was three days before the new moon, which rose shortly after midnight.

[2] Lt.-Col. Alexander MacDonald, Portree, a great-grand-nephew of Malcolm MacLeod and of Mrs. John MacKinnon, informs me that the family tradition is that the Prince went round to the west to avoid Portree and then turned south. To avoid Sligachan, then occupied by the enemy, he skirted the very top of the loch of that name, and reached Elgol by the circuitous route of Strath Mohr.

[3] The tradition of the site is carefully preserved, but the house no longer exists.

[4] A cave, Uamh Phrionnsa, on the beach where the Prince is said to have awaited the boat, is still shown.

[5] Alexander MacDonald says they landed at Buarblach, a few miles further south (I. 332), but MacKinnon, who was with the Prince, is entirely corroborated by tradition, according to which he landed in the middle of the Mallaig Harbour, not very far from where the projected railway terminus will be. The tradition of his sleeping in the open air is preserved in the district, but no particular places are pointed out.

[6] The Militia were then quartered at Earnsaig on Loch Nevis (see map). The tradition is preserved that he landed at Bracken Point (*Ord. Sur.* Sron Raineach), and climbed the hill Aonach, now green sloping pastures, but then covered with trees.

July 8.   hours (II. 251, III. 183), then re-embarked and
            crossed to 'a little island about a mile from Scotus's
            house.[1] John MacKinnon landed, met old Clan-
            ranald, who refused to give assistance (III. 186);
            returned to Mallaig, whence, accompanied by old
            MacKinnon and John, the Prince walked by night
            to Morar,[2] MacDonald of Morar then living in a
            hut or bothy, as his house had been burned down
            (II. 252).

„   9.   Morar gave hospitality, and went to seek young Clan-
            ranald, then in the neighbourhood; the Prince and
            party went to a cave[3] and slept (II. 252). Morar
            returned unsuccessfully, he said, from his search
            for young Clanranald (III. 187). Morar declined to
            give any further assistance, and the party resolved
            to seek refuge with MacDonald of Borradale. In
            the evening they started, Morar sending his son as
            a guide (II. 252, III. 188).

     10.   Arrived at Borradale in early morning.[4] Found Angus
            MacDonald living in a bothy, as his house had
            been burned (II. 252).

            The old chief of MacKinnon and John MacKinnon here
            left the Prince. Both were taken prisoner the following
            day, the chief at Morar, and John, who escaped from
            Morar, when he arrived by night at Elgol (II. 253).

„ 11–12. At Borradale[5] (I. 333).

„   13.   Borradale sent his son John to summon his nephew,
            Alexander MacDonald of Glenaladale (ib.). The
            Prince hearing that MacKinnon had been captured,

---

[1] Eilean na Glaschoille, called to this day the 'Prince's Isle.'

[2] Glenaladale calls this place Cross (I. 332), which it is also called in Dorret's
map. None of it remains, but it stood in what is now a ploughed field, a long
mile south of the bridge over the Morar river.

[3] The cave is about a mile from the site of the house, near the mouth of the
river, in the face of a cliff some twenty-five feet high. It is small but deep,
and well suited for concealment. A pleasant white beach lies to the west
of the cave.

[4] Tradition still shows the cave on the shore below Borradale House which
the Prince is believed to have inhabited on this visit to Borradale [G.].

[5] From this point to August 20th, Glenaladale's narrative is followed, corro-
borated and supplemented by that of John MacDonald, Borradale's son, and
Patrick Grant, one of the Glenmoriston men.
The whole of Glenaladale's dates are, however, antedated by five days

July 13.	removed four miles to the eastward (I. 334) to MacLeod's Cove, 'upon a high precipice in the woods of Borradale' (III. 377).[1]
,, 14.	At MacLeod's Cove [2] (I. 334).
,, 15.	Glenaladale joined the Prince (*ib.*).
,, 16.	Heard from Angus MacEachine, Borradale's son-in-law, that the Prince's presence was suspected (*ib.*), and he offered a place of concealment he had prepared near Meoble, in the Braes of Morar (III. 377). Ranald MacDonald, Borradale's son, sent to examine and report on the place (I. 334).
,, 17.	John MacDonald, Borradale's son, sent to reconnoitre, 'visibly saw the whole coast surrounded by ships-of-war and tenders, as also the country by other military forces.' So the Prince started for Mac-

for the following reasons : Glenaladale, with extraordinary minuteness and lucidity, narrates the Prince's movements from the time of his crossing from Skye to the time he started to join Lochiel and Cluny in Badenoch, a period of fifty-five days, every one of which he accounts for. His accuracy, corroborated by John MacDonald and Duncan Grant, is beyond doubt ; his journal, too, was written very shortly after the event, while the facts were fresh in his memory. It will be observed that he dates the Prince's crossing from Skye to the mainland July 10th (I. 332), while the actual date of that crossing, July 5th, is one of the best authenticated dates in the whole story—a difference of five days. Beginning with that date, he carries the Prince through forty-seven days until he reaches the wood of Torvault on August 26th, in the neighbourhood of which he remained eight days (I. 349), which would bring him to September 2nd. But we know from Cluny's narrative that the Prince left Torvault for Badenoch on the 28th (III. 39) —again a difference of five days. The assumption of Glenaladale's being five days wrong throughout is further corroborated by Patrick Grant, one of the Glenmoriston men. Grant, to whom the Prince's visit was the great event of his life, and firmly fixed in his memory, is absolutely certain that Prince Charles joined him eight days before Lammas (III. 99) that is July 24th, while Glenaladale makes the date the 29th (I. 343)—once more a difference of five days. The shifting of Glenaladale's dates five days earlier throughout his entire narrative thus appears fully justified. That Bishop Forbes observed the discrepancies is evident from his remarks (III. 99) and the alteration of Glenaladale's dates that he made on the information furnished by Forbes for Finlayson's map, which differ but little from the dates which are given in this Itinerary. All discrepancies are got rid of by the hypothesis of the five days' error. Cf. additional note, p. 107 *post*.

[1] So says Glenaladale ; John MacDonald says the move took place after Glenaladale joined them.

[2] Though the tradition of MacLeod's Cove is still preserved in the district, its site is entirely lost [G.]. Even in 1746 it was 'known to very few of the country people' (I. 334). Cf. III. 191.

July 17.   Eachine's refuge [1] without waiting for Ranald's re-
                  turn, attended by Glenaladale, Borradale, and his
                  son John. Walking to Corrybeincabir (*Ord. Sur.*
                  Ben-nan-cabar), the party met MacEachine and
                  learned from him that young Clanranald was within
                  a few miles of them, and that he had prepared a
                  'safe place' for the Prince. As it was too late to
                  go to him this night, the party went on to Meoble
                  (III. 377) and spent the night there, intending to
                  join Clanranald next day. Hearing that General
                  Campbell was in Loch Nevis with a large force,
                  naval and military, they sent two men to
                  reconnoitre, and Borradale returned to procure
                  necessaries (I. 335).

,,   18.   Borradale brought news in the early morning that
                  Clanranald's country was surrounded. In fact a
                  line of camps and sentries had been established
                  from the head of Loch Eil to the head of Loch
                  Hourn (I. 338, II. 364), the enemy evidently
                  having learned that the Prince had landed in
                  Moidart. It was now impossible to join young
                  Clanranald, so the party resolved to skirt the line
                  of posts, break through them somewhere, and make
                  for Poolewe or some port farther north. The
                  Prince set out, accompanied by Glenaladale, his
                  brother John, and John MacDonald, Borradale's
                  son. At mid-day they reached Scoorvuy (*Ord.
                  Sur.* Sgur Mhuide), whence they sent Glenala-
                  dale's brother to Glenfinnan for news, and arranged
                  to meet at Scoorwick Corrichan (*Ord. Sur.* Sgor nan
                  Coireachan). At two o'clock reached Fruighvein
                  (*Ord. Sur.* Fraoch-bheinn), where, finding some
                  clansmen and learning that the troops were rigour-
                  ously searching the country which they had sur-
                  rounded, Donald Cameron of Glenpean was sent for
                  to guide the party out of Moidart. Hearing that
                  troops had reached the foot of the hill they were on,

---

[1] This place, though not shown on the Ordnance maps, is well known to
the people of the district. It is high up the Corry, about half-a-mile west of
the small loch Torr na h Airidh, and about a mile north of the west end of
Locheilt [G.]. On this map it is figured 'MacEachine's Refuge.'

July 18.   they could not wait till Glenpean came, but started at sunset and accidentally met him, about eleven o'clock, at Corrour,[1] in the Braes of Morar (III. 377), and walked with him all night (I. 337).

> *On July 18th Cumberland left Fort Augustus for England, leaving Lord Albemarle as Commander-in-Chief[2]* (S.M. 342).

„   19.   Arrived in the morning at top of Mamnyn Callum [3] in the Brae of Loch Arkaig, which, having been searched the day before, they judged safe, and spent the day there. Here they were accidentally joined by Glenaladale's brother, whom they had not been able to meet at Corrichan, as arranged. They left at nine at night (I. 338).

„   20.   Reached Corringagaull (*Ord. Sur.* Coire-nan-gall) at 1 A.M., hoping to find clansmen, but finding none, went on to 'a fast place' at the head of Loch Quoich, a mile off (I. 339). Young Glenaladale, sent to find provisions, returned at three o'clock to say that troops were marching up the other side of the hill. The party started at eight o'clock, climbed to top of Drimachosi (*Ord. Sur.* Druim Cosaidh), and observed the enemy's camps close to them (I. 339).

„   21.   Passed between two of the guards in Glen Cosaidh in the early morning, thus breaking through the cordon that surrounded Moidart (I. 339, II. 363). This night the Prince narrowly escaped falling over

---

[1] Corrour (*Ord. Sur.* Coire Odhar), the dun corry, is in the valley of the A. a' Choire, which runs into the east end of Loch Beoraid, and is situated about a mile south-west of the summit of Sgor nan Coireachan [G.].

[2] The general disposition of the Government troops at this time is given in S.M. 342. An idea of how the Highlands were covered with a network of small garrisons as late as 1749-50, and the details of their situations may be gathered from the reports printed in H.P.J. 513-584.

[3] Mamnynleallum in the text, a mistranscription for Mamnyn Callum (which it is called in L.P. 551 and on Finlayson's map) is without doubt a phonetic spelling of the Mam (elevated moorland) or shoulder of the Sgor Choileam of the Ordnance map. It is a pass down the slope of that high peaked hill, with a hollow running longitudinally through it capable of screening a party who might desire to proceed without being observed [G.].

July 21.   a precipice (I. 318, III. 11, 91). Reached **Corriscor-ridill** (*Ord. Sur.* Coire-Sgoir-adail), at the head of Loch Hourn, where they spent the day in ' a bit hollow ground covered with long heather and branches of young birch bushes ' (III. 378). Glenpean not knowing the country towards Poolewe, he and Glenaladale set out to look for a new guide, but, finding that they had all day been close to two camps of the enemy, they set out at night—'the darkest night ever in my life I travelled'[1] (III. 378)—without a guide, for Glenshiel,[2] in Seaforth's country (I. 340).

,,   22.   Arrived in Glenshiel in the early morning, ' and passed the whole day, which was exceeding hot, in the face of a mountain above a river that ran through Glenshiel '[3] (III. 378). Here they received refreshment from Gilchrist MacGrath[4] (or M'Kra). Finding on inquiry that the only French ship that had been at Poolewe had gone away, the Prince abandoned his intention of going there meantime, and having met Donald MacDonald, a Glengarry man, able to guide them, they resolved to seek shelter for a while in Glenmoriston, and bade farewell to Donald Cameron of Glenpean. Shortly after starting, the dramatic incident occurred of losing the purse, by going back to recover which they avoided the certainty of meeting an armed party of the enemy (I. 342).

,,   23.   Arrived in early morning at a hillside above Strath-

---

[1] Strange to say, it was the night of the full moon, which would doubtless strengthen the feeling of miraculous intervention in the Prince's escape.

[2] The natural, indeed the only practicable pass from Loch Hourn to Glenshiel is by Coire Mhalagain, and the path is in common use to this day. The most likely place to have met MacGrath was Mhalagain, which was then a township.

[3] A cave, or rather a recess under a big stone, is still pointed out as the Prince's resting-place in Glenshiel. It is a little to the east of the farm of Achnacart, shown on the map, and on the north side of the glen.

[4] Home tells a story (H.H. 252) of suspicion of intended treachery on the part of M'Kra which induced the party to turn to Glenmoriston. This has no foundation in any of the documents I have seen. The evidence is the other way. John MacDonald, who wrote his story long after the event, speaks of him as ' the honest M'Kra ' (III. 378).

THE CAVE IN GLENMORISTON

VIEW OF OPENING LOOKING DOWN THE GLEN

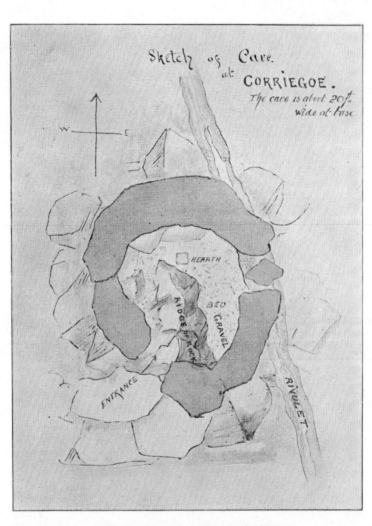

Sketch of Cave.
at CORRIEGOE.
The cave is about 20ft.
wide at base

W — E

HEARTH

RIDGE OF ROCK

BED GRAVEL

ENTRANCE

RIVULET

THE CAVE IN GLENMORISTON

GROUND-PLAN

July 23.   clunie, and rested in 'a fast place,' where they
                 spent the day, covering the Prince with heather
                 to keep off the midges (III. 379). Proceeding in the
                 afternoon, and hearing firing near them, they turned
                 northward, climbing to the top of a high hill be-
                 tween Glenmoriston and Strathglass (*Ord. Sur.*
                 Sgurr-nan-Conbhairean, *probably*). Spent the night
                 in an open cave, in which the Prince, wet to the
                 skin, could neither lean nor sleep (I. 343).

„   24.   Joined the 'famous' Glenmoriston men[1] at Coiraghoth
                 in the Braes of Glenmoriston, where the Prince was
                 lodged in a cave, 'with the finest purling stream that
                 could be running by his bedside within the grotto'
                 (I. 344); 'as comfortably lodged as if he had been
                 in a royal palace' (III. 381).

„   25—27.   At Coiraghoth[2] (I. 343).

„   28—31.   Moved on the 28th, two miles off, to Coirmheadhain
                 (*Ord. Sur.* Coire Mheadhoin) (*ib.*) or Coirskreoch
                 (III. 99) and resided in 'a grotto no less romantic
                 than the former,' for four days (I. 344).

---

[1] For the names of these eight faithful robbers, see III. 202.

[2] Coiraghoth, as it is spelt by Glenaladale, is a phonetic rendering of the
Gaelic Coiredhogha, the last three letters of which are silent, or pronounced as
a grunt, while the 'dh' has a guttural sound. It means the corry of the river
Doe, of which the stream of the Coire Mheadhoin is an affluent. Home spells it
Corado (H. H. 253), and Mr. Ross calls it Corriegoe.

I have been singularly fortunate in obtaining the sketches of this celebrated
cave which embellish this volume from Mr. Ross, formerly Provost of Inverness,
who made them when on a visit to this wild and inaccessible district in July 1888.

Mr. Ross's description in a letter to myself entirely corroborates that of
Glenaladale. ' . . . a cavern formed by the great masses of rock at the bottom
of a talus from the hill above—in fact a cavity in a cairn of stones. The roof of
the cavity is formed by a peculiarly shaped mass, very much resembling three-
quarters of an umbrella resting on a spur of rock. The floor of the cave takes
a crescent form, the entrance being at the south-west, and coming round by
the north to the south-east. About the centre was what appeared to be a
hearth, and the south-east would have formed the bed. The bottom of the
cavern was of gravel, and a pure rivulet of water passed close under the east
side of the cave.'

Glenaladale mentions two caves in Glenmoriston, but only one is now
known, and one of my informants, a gamekeeper of the district, stoutly denies
that there can be two. Although John of Borradale only mentions one cave
(III. 381), I firmly believe in Glenaladale's accuracy, and that a second 'grotto
no less romantic than the former' really exists, although its site, like that of
MacLeod's cove, may have been lost.

July 31.   *On July 27th Kingston's Horse left Fort Augustus for England* (S.M. 392).

Aug. 1.   Learning that Captain Campbell of the Militia was encamped within four miles of them, resolved to move northward, travelling by night (I. 344).

„   2.   In early morning arrived in Chisholm's country, the Braes of Strathglass, lodging in 'a sheally hut'[1] (I. 345).

---

[1] The route from Coire Mheadoin to Strathglass and the resting-places in Chisholm's country are traditional and conjectural. There is no direct evidence in any contemporary narrative, and minute local investigation has failed to elucidate any very satisfactory traditional information. The most likely route on the journey north would be over the shoulder of Tigh Mohr into the pass of Alt na Ciche, which debouches into Glen Affrick at Ardnamulloch, at the head of Loch Affrick, and thence down Glen Affrick to the fast places of Fasnakyle—Chisholm's woods. The woods in this district are eminently suited for such a shelter as is described by John MacDonald (III. 381). Local tradition has it that the Prince's principal shelter in Strathglass was at the Achans, a hamlet on the eastern slope of the Beinn Acherain of the *Ord. Sur.*, and here probably the shieling described by John MacDonald was erected. From his narrative, written however long after the event, one would imagine that the party was stationary while in Chisholm's country, and possibly John remained in this refuge while the Prince and Glenaladale impatiently followed the road towards Poolewe in hopes of intelligence, as narrated by Glenaladale. There is some ambiguity, too, in Glenaladale's narrative, supplemented by Patrick Grant's (I. 346, III. 99), about climbing the hill Peinachyrine (or Beinn Acharain). Glenaladale says the party climbed a hill on the north side of Glen Cannich, which Patrick Grant says was called Peinachyrine, while the modern Beinn Acharain of the Ordnance Survey is on the south side of that glen. Grant says this was the most northerly point attained by the party. Now, if the modern map be right, one or other of these companions of the Prince must be in error. I think, however, that it is the modern map that does not correspond with the names of 1746. Loch Bunacharan (*Ord. Sur.*) is in Glen Strathfarrar to the North of Glen Cannich. The name signifies the foot of Acharan, and I think there can be no doubt that the mountain which the Prince climbed was one of the peaks overlooking this loch, and could indeed have been none other than that called in the *Ord. Sur.* Meallan Odhar, which rises behind Leitry, and on Dorret's map of Scotland (1750) is actually figured Binachren.* This would of course be positive proof, were it not that Dorret's map is very incorrect in its topographical details of this part of the country. On Arrowsmith's Map (1807) and in Thomson's County Atlas (1832), in both of which the topography is fairly correct, neither the mountain now called Meallan Odhar nor that now called Beinn Acharain in the *Ord. Sur.* is named at all, though both are shown. The Prince's object in climbing the hill was to meet his messenger returning from Poolewe, which would be attained by his going up this *Ord. Sur.* Meallan Odhar, while

---

* In Blaeu's map of 1662, in which the topography is more correct than in Dorret's, and in Moll's atlas of 1725 the range is called 'Skurr na Corran.'

Aug. 3. Remained in the same place (I. 345).

  „   4. In early morning set out northward to get nearer
          Poolewe, whence the Prince expected tidings or help,
          travelled five or six miles and spent the night in 'a
          sheally hut' (*ib.*). Hence the Prince despatched
          two of the party to Poolewe, 40 Highland miles off.

  „   5. In early morning started, still travelling north, arrived
          at mid-day at Glencanna (*Ord. Sur.* Glencannich),
          passed the rest of the day in a wood, and late at
          night got shelter in a neighbouring village (*ib.*).

  „   6. Leaving Glencannich at 2 A.M., climbed the hill
          Peinachyrine (Beinn Acharain), the most northerly
          point the Prince reached in his wanderings
          (III. 99). In the evening they repaired to 'a neigh-
          bouring sheally hut' (I. 346).

  „   7. Remained at the same place, where his messenger
          returned and informed him that the only French
          ship that had been at Poolewe had gone off, having
          landed two French officers who were making their

---

there would have been no object in climbing the Beinn Acharain of the *Ord. Sur.*
Moreover he was actually seen descending this mountain according to the narrative
of an eyewitness, apparently authentic, quoted in the Appendix to the *Lays of the
Deer Forest*, vol. II. p. 343, Edinburgh, 1848. This witness actually saw the
Prince: 'When first he observed him he was descending the hill at a place
called Ruigh an t-Stucain [*Ord. Sur.* Allt Liath Ruighe], a part of the farm of
Leitrie. From the direction in which the Prince descended, it was not doubted
that he had crossed over from Ard-chuilc in Glen-Strathfarrar, which is exactly
opposite to the farm of Leitrie, on the side of the Loch of Beinachrine [Ard-chuilc
is really on the side of Loch a Mhuilinn, a small loch a little above Bunacharan],
and in the ordinary track of a person crossing the hill from Poll-Eu.'
    The authors of the *Lays* go on to argue that the Prince had visited Glen Strath-
farrar, and point to a traditional cave near Deannie, on the northern side of
the glen, as one of the Prince's hiding-places.   But for this there is no
authority whatever; on the contrary, the direct evidence of Patrick Grant is that
the Prince never visited Glen Strathfarrar (III. 101), though he overstates his
case by saying that he was never within seven miles of it, as all Glen Cannich is
nearer than that. I have assumed the hill above Leitry, where he was actually
seen, as the farthest north of his wanderings, and have shown it so on this
map. There is a cave called Craig Feasaig near Leitry, traditionally a refuge of
the Prince. It is quite possible he was there, but there is no evidence for it,
and all caves near where he was known to have travelled have a way of
developing myths.
    Tradition also states that the Prince spent a night in Comar, a house
belonging to the Chisholm, but for this too I can procure no authority.

Aug. 7. way for Lochiel's country in search of the Prince. He accordingly abandoned his idea of going to Poolewe and resolved to go south again, hoping to meet them and get their despatches (I. 346).

,, 8. At night [1] started off towards Strathglass. Crossed the Cannich water, and 'boldly by young Chisholm's house' [2] (*ib.*).

,, 9. In early morning reached Fasnacoill (*Ord. Sur.* Fasnakyle), and remained three days 'in a very fast wood' (*ib.*).

,, 10–11. At Fasnacoill. Getting information that the troops who had been searching for the Prince had gone back to Fort Augustus, they resolved to go on (*ib.*).

,, 12. Set out in the morning and in four hours reached the Braes of Glenmoriston,[3] passed the day on the top of a hill, and learning that a strong party was scouring the Braes of Glengarry they resolved to wait till the road was clear and spent the night in a 'neighbouring sheally hut' (*ib.*).

,, 13. Sent a messenger to see if Glengarry were clear of troops and two to Loch Arkaig to summon Cameron of Clunes (*ib.*).

> On 13th August Albemarle's camp at Fort Augustus was broken up, and the main body of the army marched southwards (S. M. 393).
>
> Campbell's Argyleshire militia were marched to Inveraray and disbanded on the 17th. Lord Loudon was left with his own regiment and seventeen companies of militia (ib. 374).

,, 14. Learning from their messenger that the road was clear, the Prince and his party 'ten in number'[4] starting in the afternoon passed through Glenmoriston and Glenlyne to Glengarry, forded the Garry with difficulty and spent the night about a mile from the stream on the 'side of a hill, without any cover, though it rained excessively' (I. 347).

---

[1] There could have been no moonlight. The moon set shortly after sunset.

[2] Almost certainly Muchrachd, then a residence of the Chisholm, but the party must have passed the house before fording the Cannich.

[3] To reach Glenmoriston from Strathglass in four hours, the route taken must have been that shown in the map, by Guisachan and Loch-na-Beinne-Baine.

[4] The ten were the Prince, Glenaladale, his brother John, young John of Borradale, and six of the Glenmoriston men, the other two having been sent to Loch Arkaig.

Aug. 15.   Travelled six miles across the hills to the Brae of Achnasual. Passed the day in ' a most inconvenient habitation, it raining as heavily within as without it.' The messengers returned here from Clunes with instructions to go to a wood two miles off where he would meet them next day. They found it to be 'a very fast place.'[1] (Here occurred the incident of shooting the stag, when they were entirely destitute of food (I. 96).) They were joined this night by MacDonald of Lochgarry (I. 348), and [probably] by Cameron of Achnasual and Captain MacRaw of Glengarry's Regiment (I. 96).

„ 16.   At Loch Arkaig.[1] Joined by Cameron of Clunes, who took them to a wood at the foot of Loch Arkaig[2] (I. 348).

„ 17.   At Loch Arkaig. The Prince sent John MacPherson or M'Colvain to summon Lochiel (ib., III. 39).

„ 18–19. At Loch Arkaig (I. 348).

„ 20.   Dr. Cameron, Lochiel's brother, accompanied by the Rev. John Cameron, arrived with Lochiel's apology for not coming himself (I. 96, 349).

„ 21.   On the 21st moved to the wood of Torvault[3] a mile off, opposite Achnacarie (I. 349). [Probably] this was the day that the Prince, disguised as Captain Drummond, received the two French officers (I. 98, 349, III. 102) who came with Dr. Cameron, read their despatches, but found nothing of importance. Dr. Cameron, Lochgarry, and Clunes left (I. 349), and [probably] young Glenaladale and young Borradale returned to the west coast to look out for French ships (III. 382).

„ 22.   At Torvault (I. 349).

„ 23.   [Probably] the French officers left.[4] [Probably] this day the Prince was surprised by a party of Loudon's

---

[1] The present Lochiel informs me that this 'fast place' is a cave about two miles east of Achnasual, in the wood of Torre Chrone, on the left bank of the stream flowing through Glen Cia-aig, to the north of the dark mile (*Ord. Sur.* Mile Dorcha), about a mile from the east end of Loch Arkaig.

[2] This second shelter was probably near Clunes House, at the east end of the same wood.

[3] This third shelter (the three are specially mentioned, I. 99) was in the wood erroneously called Tor Gallain in the *Ord. Sur.*, now spelt Torvoult.

[4] They remained two days at Torvault (I. 99).

Aug. 23.   regiment under Grant of Knockando who discovered the hut in Torvault.[1] The Prince retired to the top of the hill Mullantagart[2] (*Ord. Sur.* Meall-an-Tagraidh), in the Braes of Glen Kingie, where he remained all night (I. 100).

  „ 24.   [Probably] the Prince slept in the forenoon on the mountain-top, in his wet clothes wrapped in his plaid, in spite of cold and hail. Spent the night in the strath of Glen Kingie (*ib.*).

  „ 25.   [Probably] at the same place[3] (*ib.*).

  „ 26.   [Probably] returned to the Braes of Achnacarie (*ib.*). [Probably] this day the Glenmoriston men, with the exception of Patrick Grant, were dismissed (III. 101).[4]

---

[1] There has been considerable difficulty in fitting in the details of this adventure as narrated by the Rev. John Cameron. The story is told with great vagueness and with obvious inaccuracy, both as to time and place. His date of August 10 (I. 99), is an impossible one; the incident could only have happened after they had been a few days at Torvault, and before Dr. Cameron and Lochgarry returned from Badenoch. It is remarkable that neither Glenaladale nor Cluny nor Patrick Grant mentions Mr. Cameron's name, or alludes in the slightest way to his story, or to his presence with the Prince; yet when Cameron's notes were shown to Glenaladale, though he said that they were 'prodigious uncorrect' (II. 366), he did not deny them; and Patrick Grant, to whom also they were read, gave a negative assent to the story (III. 102). The story was implicitly believed and accepted at the time, and is included in Home's *History*, the *Scots Magazine*, and in many of the numerous anonymous narratives of the adventures of the Prince that were printed about that time.

Glenaladale's situation at this period is a little obscure. The natural inference from the narratives would be that, on handing over the Prince to the Camerons, Glenaladale took his leave (I. 97, C.F.M. 258); but he himself relates that he did not leave Loch Arkaig until September 3rd (*i.e.* in our reckoning August 29th; *see* p. 56 note 5, *ante*), which corresponds to the morning after the Prince left for Badenoch. It is probable that on arriving at Torvault he retired from immediate attendance, but remained in the neighbourhood until the Prince left for Badenoch. Under no hypothesis will the different narratives exactly fit in, but the probable sequence of incident here given cannot be far wrong.

Both Browne and Chambers call Mr. Cameron, 'Lochiel's brother,' which appears a mistake. Lochiel's brother John was the laird of Fassefern.

[2] This hill is at the head of Glen Ci-aig, on the watershed between Loch Arkaig and Glen Garry, of which Glen Kingie is part, but the hill is a long way from the modern Glen Kingie. The term 'braes' evidently took in a large district. The Prince no doubt climbed the hill and spent the night in some shelter, on the northern side of the hill, which I have been unable to trace.

[3] Cameron says they 'lived there merrily for some days,' but it is impossible the party could have been there more than two nights, the 24th and 25th. Cameron is very vague in his narrative.

[4] They left three days before Glenaladale (III. 101).

Aug. 27.   Lochgarry and Dr. Cameron arrived from Lochiel to conduct the Prince to Badenoch (I. 101, III. 39).

,, 28.   Set out at night for Badenoch [1] accompanied by Lochgarry, Dr. Cameron, and Rev. John Cameron (I. 101, III. 39). Before crossing the Lochy, the Prince bade farewell to Patrick Grant, the Glenmoriston man, giving him twenty-four guineas for his friends (III. 102). On the journey to Badenoch, MacDonell of Tullochcrom met the Prince and presented him with some clothes and shoes (III. 182).

---

[1] This is a long journey of over thirty miles, and probably occupied the night of the 28th and the whole of the 29th. There would have been ample moonlight if the night were clear, as the moon was in her last quarter and rose about half-past nine.

The only narrative that I have been able to find which gives an indication of the Prince's route from Loch Arkaig to Badenoch is that of Lochgarry, printed as postscript to this Itinerary. From it we learn that after crossing the Lochy (III., 102) the party proceeded by the eastern side of the line of lochs now forming the Caledonian Canal, to 'within two short miles of Fort Augustus.' From this point it is necessary to fall back partly on conjecture, and partly on local tradition. Probably the party, after approaching Fort Augustus, turned up Glen Tarff, crossed the shoulder of Carn Leac, and passed by the watershed dividing the Spey from the Roy to the ridge of Craig Meggie (Creag Meaghaidh), where tradition says the Prince was met by Alexander MacDonell of Tullochcrom, and this agrees with MacDonell's own statement that he met the Prince 'just on his entering Badenoch' (III. 182). Tradition says that the Prince was conducted down 'the window of Coire Arder' to the house of Aberarder on Loch Laggan, and was there entertained by Ranald MacDonell, Tullochcrom's brother, then tacksman of Aberarder. Tradition is strong on that point, yet it is almost impossible to believe that a visit to Aberarder House really took place. Not only is there no reference to such a visit in Cluny's or in Lochgarry's narrative, but when, in 1760, after all danger was over, the brothers met Bishop Forbes in Leith (III. 182), undoubtedly with a view of telling all they knew, no mention is made of a visit to Aberarder. After Culloden the Tullochcrom family had made their peace with Loudon, and one of the brothers was nominally employed in searching for the Prince; and although, instead of capturing, they secretly assisted him, I cannot believe, without further authority, that they would have actually brought him to their house on Loch Laggan side, only a few miles from Loudon's camps at Dalwhinny and Garvemore; and still less that the brothers would have concealed the visit from Bishop Forbes, though in this the Rev. Mr. Sinton of Dores, to whom I am indebted for much in these notes, does not agree with me. It seems to me far more likely that the tradition has grown around the recorded fact that the MacDonells fed and clothed the Prince on his journey, and that he was not very far from Aberarder. Mr. Sinton perfectly remembers old people telling how he came down Coire Arder, and was under the protection of the MacDonells.

Aug. 29.   Reached Corrineuir [1] at the foot of Benalder (III. 39).

„   30.   Reached Mellaneuir [1] 'a shieling of very narrow compass,' where he met Lochiel, whose companions were MacPherson of Breakachie, Cluny's brother-in-law; Allan Cameron, a cadet of Cullan, and two of Cluny's servants (*ib.*).

„   31.   At Mellaneuir (III. 41).

Sept. 1.   Cluny joined the party at Mellaneuir (*ib.*).

„   2.   Moved to Uiskchilra [2] (*Ord. Sur.* Allt a Chaoil Reidhe), two miles further into Benalder, to 'a little shiel . . . superlatively bad and smokey' (*ib.*)

„   3–4.   At Uiskchilra 'two or three nights' (*ib.*).

„   5.   Moved two miles further into the mountain to Cluny's 'Cage' in the face of 'a very rough high rocky mountain called Letternilichk [3] which is still a part of Benalder' (III. 42).

---

[1] Corrineuir and Mellaneuir are phonetic spellings of the hill called on the Ordnance Survey maps Mullah Coire an Iubhair (the bh is silent), part of the Benalder range. Corrineuir is the *Ord. Sur.* Coire an Iubhair Mór on the north-east slope of the hill, and Mellaneuir most probably the Mealan Odhar of the *Ord. Sur.*, on the south-east slope of the hill, on a track half a mile west of Loch Pattack.

[2] A phonetic spelling of Uisge Chaoil Reidhe which is synonymous with the *Ord. Sur.* Allt a Chaoil Reidhe, meaning the stream of the narrow meadow.

[3] Letternilichk is a phonetic rendering of Litir-na-lic, 'the slope of the slab of stone,' litir being a slope rising from a sheet of water. There is a certain amount of obscurity about the exact site of Cluny's Cage. Tradition has grown up round a cave above Ben Alder Lodge, near the south-western end of Loch Ericht, figured on the *Ord. Sur.* as Prince Charles's Cave. Yet it is not quite certain that this was the veritable site of the Cage, the tradition of which is well known to the shepherds and gamekeepers of the district. The Cage was an artificial structure of two storeys (1), on a southern spur of Ben Alder (2), overlooking Loch Ericht (3), on the face of a rocky hill (4), in a thicket of holly (5), so situated that sentries could give warning (6). It was never discovered by the enemy. All traces of the shanty have naturally disappeared, but the site of the cave fulfils the necessary conditions, excepting that of the thicket of holly; yet, as trees have disappeared in many parts of the Highlands, the holly may have died out here. The following description, from an account of the visit of the Cairngorm Club in 1894, is printed in the Club's *Journal*, Aberdeen, Jan. 1895: 'It is an exceedingly rude shelter, consisting of several large boulders tilted up at various angles, and affording the most scanty accommodation. It is divided into an upper and lower shelter, which have been fancifully designated kitchen and bedroom. [This seems to preserve the tradition of the two-storied shanty.] In some respects, the identification of it as the ill-starred Prince's hiding-place seems very probable. It affords an excellent outlook, is inaccessible, and is one of the most unlikely places in the kingdom

Sept. 6.   Two French ships having on board Colonel Warren
and Young Sheridan arrived at Lochnanuagh.

„   6-12. Remained in the Cage attended by Lochiel, Cluny,
Lochgarry, Dr. Cameron, Breakachie, Allan
Cameron, and four MacPhersons, servants of
Cluny (III. 48).

„   13.   At one o'clock in the morning, hearing of the arrival
of the ships in Lochnanuagh, the party started
for the coast. Spent the day at Uiskchilra where
he was joined by Breakachie and John Roy
Stewart. Started again at night (III. 44).

---

for prince or peasant to abide in.' The following description, from a manuscript
in the Cluny charter-chest, believed to be written about the year 1756, while
Cluny was in France [Cluny went to France in 1755, and died at Dunkirk,
Jan. 30, 1764], gives a graphic and most circumstantial account of the Cage.
It should be compared with that given in the *Lyon in Mourning*, III. 42.

' About five miles to the south-westward of his (Cluny's) chateau commenc'd
his forrest of Ben Alder, plentifully stock'd with dear—red hares, moorfoul, and
other game of all kinds, beside which it affords fine pasture for his numberous
flocks and heards. There also he keeps a harras of some hundred mares, all
which after the fatal day of Culoden became the pray of his enemies. It contains
an extent of many mountains and small valleys, in all computed about 12
miles long east and west, and from 8 to 10 miles in breadth, without a single
house in the whole excepting the necessary lodges for the shepherds who were
charg'd with his flocks. It was in this forrest where the Prince found Cluny with
Locheill in his wounds and other friends under his care. He was afraid that his
constitution might not suit with lying on the ground or in caves, so was solicitous
to contrive a more comfortable habitation for him upon the south front of one of
these mountains, overlooking a beautifull lake of 12 miles long. He observed
a thicket of hollywood, he went, viewed and found it fit for his purpose; he
caused immediately wave the thicket round with boughs, made a first and second
floor in it, and covered it with moss to defend the rain. The uper room serv'd
for *salle à manger* and bed chamber while the lower serv'd for a cave to contain
liquors and other necessaries, at the back part was a proper hearth for cook and
baiker, and the face of the mountain had so much the colour and resemblance of
smock, no person cou'd ever discover that there was either fire or habitation in
the place. Round this lodge were placed their sentinels at proper stations, some
nearer and some at greater distances, who dayly brought them notice of what
happened in the country, and even in the enemie's camps, bringing them likewise the necessary provisions, while a neighbouring fountain supplied the society
with the rural refreshment of pure rock water. As, therefore, an oak tree is to
this day rever'd in Brittain for having happily sav'd the grand uncle, Charles the
Second, from the pursuits of Cromwell so this holly thicket will probablie in
future times be likeways rever'd for having saved Prince Charles, the nephew,
from the still more dangerous pursuits of Cumberland, who show'd himself on
all occasions a much more inveterate enemy. In this romantick humble habita-

Sept.	14.	Reached Corvoy[1] by daylight and rested during the day, going on in the evening to Uisknifichit (*Ord. Sur.* Uisge-nam-Fichead) on the confines of Glenroy, where they slept, starting again before daylight (III. 44).
,,	15.	Got over Glenroy before dawn and kept themselves private all day (III. 44).
.,	16.	During the night crossed the Lochy and reached Achnacarie,[2] where they spent the day and started again by night (III. 45).
,,	17.	Reached Glencamger (*Ord. Sur.* Camgharaidh)[3] in the head of Loch Arkaig, where they met Cluny and Dr. Cameron, who had gone on to prepare for them, and to obtain provisions from a private dépôt in Coilerig (*Ord. Sur.* Collarig) of Glenroy. Spent the night here (III. 46).
,,	18.	Travelled all day towards Borradale (*ib.*).
,,	19.	Reached Borradale, where the Prince and a large number of his followers embarked[4] on board a French ship[5] (I. 319).
,,	20.	Weighed anchor shortly after midnight of the 19th and sailed to France (III. 52).

---

tion the Prince dwelt. When news of the ships being arrived reached him Cluny convoyed him to them with joy happy in having so safely plac'd so valuable a charge ; then returned with contentment, alone to commence his pilgrimage, which continued for nine years more. And now, notwithstanding the very great difference of his present situation and circumstances to what they once were, he is always gay and chearfull ; conscious of having done his duty, he defys fortune to make him express his mind unhappy, or so much as make him think of any action below his honour.'

[1] Corvoy is a phonetic rendering of the genitive of ' Moy ' (*Gaelic* Coir-a Mhaighe), the corry of the Moy burn.

[2] Achnacarie House had been burned down by Cumberland's soldiers on May 28th (S.M. 287).

[3] A letter in the Cluny charter-chest from the Prince to Cluny, dated Diralagich, in Glencamgier, 18th Sept., is facsimile'd in Mr. Macpherson's *Church and Social Life in the Highlands*, Edinburgh, 1893, and in S.N.M., in the latter of which it is erroneously stated that the Prince used New Style dates.

[4] A letter from the Prince to Cluny, written on board ship, and dated the 20th, ordering disbursements of £150 to Glengarry's clansmen, £300 to Lochiel's, £100 each to the Macgregors and the Stewarts, £100 to Lady Keppoch, and £100 to Cluny himself, is partially facsimile'd in S.N.M., p. 143.

[5] See additional note, p. 102.

APPENDIX
AND
ADDITIONAL
NOTES

APPENDIX

THE PRINCE AND LORD GEORGE MURRAY

Most of the following Letters from the Stuart Papers at Windsor and the Record Office, London, showing how strained the relations became between the Prince and Lord George Murray, are, I believe, published for the first time.

LORD GEORGE MURRAY TO THE PRINCE[1]

Jan. y⁶ 6ᵗʰ 1746.

IT is proposed that His Royal Highness shou'd from time to time call a Council of War to consist of all those who command Battalions or Squadrons ; but as severals of those may be on partys, and often absent, a Committee should be chosen by those Commanders, to consist of five or seven, and that all Operations for the carrying on the War shou'd be agreed on, by the Majority of those in His Royal Highness presence, and once that a Measure is taken, it is not to be changed except by the advice of those, or most of them, who were present when it was agreed on.

That upon any sudden Emergency such as in a Battle, Skirmish, or in a Siege, a Discretionary power must be allowed to those who command. This is the Method of all Armys, and where so many Gentlemen of Fortune, not only venture their own and their Familys All, But if any Misfortune happen are sure of ending their lives on a Scaffold should they escape in the field, if this plan is not followed the most Dismal Consequence cannot but ensue.

Had not a Council determined the Retreat from Derby, what

---

[1] State Papers Domestic, George II. This letter and the reply in the Record Office are probably copies, possibly by Sheridan. The original, in Lord George's handwriting, with the reply in the Prince's own handwriting, are in the possession of the Duke of Atholl. The original bears an endorsement in Lord George's hand, which states that he gave it to the Prince himself, and next day the proposal was sent back with the answer written on the same paper in H.R.H. own hand (A.).

a Catastrophy must have followed in two or three Days! Had a Council of War been held the Army came to Lancaster, a Day (which at that time was so precious) had not been lost. Had a Council of War been consulted as to the leaving a Garrison at Carlisle it would never have been agreed to, the place not being tenable, and so many brave men wou'd not have been sacrifized, besides the reputation of his Royal Highness Arms.

It is to be considered that this Army is an Army of Volunteers, and not Mercenarys, many of them being resolved not to continue in the Army, were affairs once settled.   GEORGE MURRAY.

THE PRINCE'S REPLY[1]

WHEN I came into Scotland I knew well enough what I was to expect from my Ennemies, but I little foresaw what I meet with from my Friends. I came vested with all the Authority the King cou'd give me, one chief part of which is the Command of his Armies, and now I am required to give this up to fifteen or sixteen Persons, who may afterwards depute five or seven of their own number to exercise it, for fear if they were six or eight that I might myself pretend to ye casting vote. By the majority of these all things are to be determined, and nothing left to me but the honour of being present at their debates. This I am told is the method of all Armies and this I flatly deny, nor do I believe it to be the Method of any one Army in the World. I am often hit in the teeth that this is an Army of Volunteers, and consequently very different from one composed of Mercenarys. What one wou'd naturally expect from an Army whose chief Officers consist of Gentlemen of rank and fortune, and who came into it meerly upon Motives of Duty and Honour, is more zeal, more resolution and more good manners than in those that fight meerly for pay: but it can be no Army at all where there is no General, or which is the same thing no Obedience or deference paid to him. Every one knew before he engaged in the cause, what he was to expect in case it miscarried, and shoud have staid at home if he coud not face Death in any shape: but can I myself hope for better usage? at least I am the only Person upon whose head a Price has been already set, and therefore I cannot indeed

---

[1] State Papers Domestic, George II. Cf. preceding note.

threaten at every other Word to throw down my Arms and make my Peace with the Government. I think I shew every day that I do not pretend to act without taking advice, and yours oftener than any body's else, which I shall still continue to do, and you know that upon more occasions than one, I have given up my own opinion to that of others. I staid indeed a day at Lancaster without calling a Council, yet y^{r}self proposed to stay another but I wonder much to see myself reproached with the loss of Carlile. Was there a possibility of carrying off the Cannon and baggage, or was there time to destroy them? and wou'd not the doing it have been a greater dishonour to our Arms? After all did not you y^{r}self instead of proposing to abandon it, offer to stay with the Athol Brigade to defend it?

I have insensibly made this answer much longer than I intended, and might yet add much more, but I choose to cut it short, and shall only tell you that my Authority may be taken from me by violence, but I shall never resign it like an Idiot.

[*Endorsed* etc.]—A Paper and Answer between Sheridan and Lord George Murray about the Authority of the Genl of the Army. Jany 6, 1746.

LORD GEORGE MURRAY TO THE PRINCE'S SECRETARY [1]

Falkirk, 29th Jany 1746.

D^R S^R,—The Gentlemen who sign the enclosed representation Intreat you would take the most prudent method to lay it before His Royall Highness without loss of time. We are sensible that it will be very unpleasant, but in the Name of God what can we do? It is as we apprehend our indispensable duty to spake our minds freely. One thing we think of the greatest Consequence, what ever His Royall Highness determine, let the thing be kept as secret as the nature of it will allow; and only those consulted who may be depended upon for their Prudence and probity.

I am D^r S^r with great esteem,
Your most Humble and Obedient Servant,
GEORGE MURRAY.

[*Endorsed*]—29 Jany 1746.

---

[1] State Papers Domestic, George II.

[The ADDRESS from the Chiefs advising the retreat to the North, dated Falkirk, 29th January, is printed as Appendix xxxix. in Home's *History*.

The reasons given are the number of desertions which are hourly increasing, the failure to take Stirling Castle, and the risk of meeting the enemy with an attenuated army. They suggest retiring immediately to the Highlands, mastering the forts of the North, and renewing the campaign in Spring. If a landing should meanwhile take place, the Highlanders would immediately rise. The Address is signed by Lord George Murray, Lochiel, Keppoch, Clanranald, Ardshiel, Lochgarry, Scotus, and the Master of Lovat.]

DECLARATION OF THE CHIEFS[1]

WE whose names are hereunto subscribed do hereby solemnly and in the Presence of God declare, that tho' for reasons which to us seem of the greatest weight we have advised His Royal Highness to retire beyond the Forth, We are still firmly resolved to stand by him and the Glorious Cause we have espoused to the utmost hazard of our lives and Fortunes.

[*No endorsement.*]

THE PRINCE TO THE CHIEFS[2]

Bannockburn, Jan. y[e] 30th.

GENTLEMEN,—I have received y[rs] of last night and am extremely surprised at the contents of it, w[ch] I little expected from you at this time. Is it possible that a Victory and a Defeat shou'd produce the same effects, and that the Conquerors should flie from an engagement, whilst the conquer'd are seeking it? Shou'd we make the retreat you propose, how much more will that raise the spirits of our Ennemys and sink those of our own People? Can we imagin, that where we go the Ennemy will not follow, and at last oblige us to a Battel which we now decline? Can we hope to defend ourselves at Perth, or keep our Men together there, better than we do here? We must therefore continue our flight to the Mountains, and soon find our selves in a worse condition than we were in at Glenfinnen. What Opinion will the French and Spaniards then have of us, or what encouragement will it be to the former to make the descent for which they have been so

---

[1] State Papers Domestic, George II.   [2] *Ibid.*

long preparing, or the latter send us any more succours? I am persuaded that if the Descent be not made before this piece of news reaches them, they will lay aside all thoughts of it, cast all the blame upon us, and say it is vain to send succours to those who dare not stay to receive them. Will they send us any more Artillery to be lost or nail'd up? But what will become of our Lowland friends? Shall we persuade them to retire with us to the Mountains? Or shall we abandon them to the fury of our Merciless Ennemies? What an Encouragement will this be to them or others to rise in our favour, shou'd we, as you seem to hope, ever think our selves in a condition to pay them a second visit? But besides what urges us to this precipitate resolution is as I apprehend the daily threats of the Ennemy to come and attack us; and if they should do it within two or three days our retreat will become impracticable. For my own Part I must say that it is with the greatest reluctance that I can bring my self to consent to such a step, but having told you my thoughts upon it, I am too sensible of what you have already ventured and done for me, not to yield to y^r unanimous resolution if you persist in it. However I must insist on the Conditions wch Sr Thomas Sheridan the Bearer of this, has my orders to propose to you. I desire you wou'd talk the matter over with him and give entire credit to what he shall say to you in my name.

Your assured friend.

[*Endorsed*]—30 Jan. 1746.

THE PRINCE TO THE CHIEFS [1]

Bannockburn, Jany 30th, 1746.

I send the Bearer Sr Thomas Sherridan in whom you all know I have entire confidence, to talk with you on the subject of your last night's memorial, as likewise to concert with you what measures shall be judged most proper to be taken at this juncture. I desire you may give entire Credit to him, and what ever shall be determined I shall readily agree to,   CHARLES, P. R.

For Lord George Murray and the heads of Clanns now att Falkirk.
[*Endorsed*]—30 Jan. 1746.

---

[1] State Papers Domestic, George II.

[Hay of Restalrig relates (Home's *History*, app. xl.) that Sheridan went to Falkirk, and returned to Bannockburn with Keppoch and several other chiefs. The following was evidently written after their interview with the Prince.]

THE PRINCE TO THE CHIEFS [1]

I DOUBT not but you have been informed by Cluny and Keppoch of what passed last night and heard great complaints of my Despotick temper, I therefore think it necessary to explain my self more fully to you. I cant see nothing but ruin and destruction to us all in case we shoud think of a retreat. Wherever we go the Ennemy will follow, and if we now appear afraid of them their spirits will rise and those of our men sink very low. I cannot conceive but we can be as well and much more safely quarter'd in and about Falkirk than here. We have already tried it for several days together, and tho' the men were order'd to be every day on the field of Battle early you know it was always near noon before they cou'd be assembled. Had the Ennemy come upon us early in ye morning, what wou'd have become of us? and shall we again wilfully put our selves in ye same risk? Believe me ye nearer we come to the Forth the greater the Desertion will prove. But this is not the worst of it. I have reason to apprehend that when we are once here it will be proposed to cross the Forth it self, in wch case we shall be utterly undon and lose all the fruits of ye success providence has hitherto granted us. Stirling will be retaken in fewer days than we have spent in taking it, and prove a second Carlile for it will be impossible to carry off our Cannon, etc. In fine why we shoud be so much afraid now of an Ennemy that we attacked and beat a fortnight ago when they were much more numerous I cannot conceive. Has the loss of so many officers and men killed and wounded and the shame of their flight still hanging upon them made them more formidable? I woud have you consider all this and represent it accordingly, but shew my letter to no mortal. After all this I know I have an Army yt I cannot command any further than the chief Officers please, and therefore if you are all resolved upon it I must yield ; but I take God to witness that it is with the greatest reluctance, and that I wash my hands of the fatal consequences wch I foresee but cannot help.

---

[1] State Papers Domestic, George II.

LORD GEORGE MURRAY TO THE PRINCE [1]

(Written from Ruthven the day after Culloden.)

MAY IT PLEASE YOUR ROYAL HIGHNESS,—As no person in these kingdomes ventured more franckly in the cause than myself and as I had more at stake than almost all the others put together, so to be sure I cannot but be very deeply affected with our late loss and present situation, but I declare that were your R.H. person in safety, the loss of the cause and the misfortunate and unhappy situation of my countrymen is the only thing that grieves me, for I thank God, I have resolution to bear my own and family's ruine without a grudge.

S[r], you will I hope upon this occasion pardon me if I mention a few truths which all the Gentlemen of our army seem convinced of.

It was highly wrong to have set up the royal standard without having positive assurance from his most Christian majesty that he would assist you with all his force, and as your royal family lost the crown of these realms upon the account of France, The world did and had reason to expect that France would seize the first favourable opportunity to restore your August family.

I must also acquaint your R.H. that we were all fully convinced that Mr. O'Sulivan whom your R.H. trusted with the most essential things with regard to your operations was exceedingly unfit for it and committed gross blunders on every occasion of moment : He whose business it was, did not so much as visit the ground where we were to be drawn up in line of Battle, and it was a fatal error yesterday to allow the enemy those walls upon their left which made it impossible for us to break them, and they with their front fire and flanking us when we went upon the attack destroyed us without any possibility of our breaking them, and our Atholl men have lost a full half of their officers and men. I wish Mr. O'Sulivan had never got any other charge in the Army than the care of the bagage which I have been told he had been brought up to and understood. I never saw him in time of Action neither at Gladsmuir, Falkirk nor in the last, and his orders were vastly confused.

The want of provisions was another misfortune which had the most fatal consequence. Mr. Hay whom Y.R.H. trusted with the

---

[1] This letter, though not included in the collection of Stuart Papers printed as an Appendix in Browne's *History*, is printed in the text of that work. The original is in Her Majesty's possession at Windsor.

The Duke of Atholl possesses a draft copy of the letter which is slightly different (A.).

principal direction of ordering provisions of late and without whose orders a boll of meal or farthing of monie was not to be delivered, has served Y.R.H. egregiously ill, when I spoke to him, he told me, the thing is ordered, it will be got etc. but he neglected his duty to such a degree that our ruin might probably been prevented had he done his duty : in short the three last days which were so critical our army was starved. This was the reason our night march was rendered abortive when we possibly might have surprised and defeat the enemy at Nairn, but for want of provisions a third of the army scattered to Inverness he and the others who marched had not spirits to make it so quick as was necessary being really faint for want of provisions.

The next day, which was the fatal day, if we had got plenty of provisions, we might have crossed the water of Nairn and drawn up so advantageously that we would have obliged the enemy to come to us, for they were resolved to fight at all hazards, at prodigious disadvantage, and probably we would in that case have done by them as they unhappily have done by us.

In short Mr. O'Sulivan and Mr. Hay had rendered themselves oddous to all our army and had disgusted them to such a degree that they had bred a mutiny in all ranks that had the battle come on they were to have represented their grievance to Y.R.H. for a remedy. For my own part I never had any particular discussion with either of them, but I ever thought them uncapable and unfit to serve in the stations they were placed in.

Y.R.H. knows I always told I had no design to continue in the army : I would of late when I came last from Atholl have resigned my commission, but all my friends told me it might be of prejudice to the cause at such a critical time. I hope your R.H. will now accept my demission. What commands you have for me in any other situation please honour me with them. I am with great zeal,

Sʳ, Your R.H. most dutifull and humble servant,

GEORGE MURRAY.

Ruthven, 17th April 1746.

[Neil MacEachain states that the Prince

'blamed always Lord George as being the only instrument in loseing the battle, and altho' that he, the morning before the action, used all his rhetorick, and eloquence against fighting, yet my Lord George out-reasoned him, 'till at last he yielded for fear to raise a dissension among the army' (N. M'E. 329).

If MacEachain has correctly reported the Prince, this means either that the generally accepted notions on the responsibility of the battle are wrong, or what is more probable, that there had been so much dissension among the Jacobite chiefs that the Prince was uncertain in his recollections as to who had given the advice to fight, and had taught himself to lay the responsibility on Lord George Murray. Lord George does not blame the Prince, but his Irish advisers (H.H. 368), and in this he is entirely corroborated by Patullo (H.H. 333). The narrative of the Rev. George Innes also states that the Prince was against fighting, though Bishop Forbes thinks that in this Innes is wrong (II. 279 and n.)]

[That the Prince in his wanderings did not express entirely hostile feelings to Lord George is evident from what he said to Kingsburgh (I. 80), which, however, a remark he made to Malcolm MacLeod a few days later goes far to neutralise (I. 135).]

[Compare also *The Lyon in Mourning*, I. 264 n, 363 n ; II. 276.]

[Apparently when the Prince got to France, his French and Irish adherents again inflamed his mind against his old commander-in-chief.]

THE PRINCE TO HIS FATHER [1]

Postscript to a letter dated ' Paris, ye 3rd Aprill 1747.'

*   *   *   *

I HAVE just received for certain àccount that L. George Murray past yᵉ Carnivall at Venice with Lord Elcho and Earl Marrichall, from thence he proceeded to Room. If it be so it is of Laste Importance he shou'd be well secured there untill He can justifie himself to me for his past Conduct, of which putting it in yᵉ best light, one will finde severall demonstrative acts of disobedience, insolency, and creating dissention: *En fin* be sides for what he deserves I humbly represent your Majesty, it wou'd be of yᵉ most Dangeross Consequences iff such a Divill was not secured immediatly in sum Castle where he might be at his ease, but without being able to escape, or have yᵉ Liberty of Pen or paper.

[*Endorsed*]—To the King, April yᵉ 3rd 1747.

[In an unpublished letter written to his father a week later (Stuart Papers), he states his opinion that, in spite of appearances, John Murray of Broughton and Lord George had been in league together.]

---

[1] From the Stuart Papers in Her Majesty's possession at Windsor, by permission.

TO THE PRINCE FROM HIS FATHER[1]

Rome, May 2, 1747

I RECEIVED by last French post My Dearest Carluccios of the 10th Aprile, and hope you will have been soon cured of your cold. One must own you are unlucky in Secretarys, but if your misfortunes are great, you have great occasions also of growing wiser by them. I should have been glad to keep L. G. Murray here until I had your answer to what I writ to you last post about him, but he is impatient to go nearer home, to be better able to look after his private affairs, and bring over his Lady, I did not think it was fit to constrain him, and so he parts in a few days, but I dont beleive he will be at Paris before the middle of June, for he goes by Venice and Switzerland; He has again spoke to me with much concern for lying under your displeasure, and if you could have seen how sincerely he ownd his faults, and how penitent he was for them, I am sure you would have been touched with it; It is certainly a very great refinement to think he has any thing to do with John Murray, nothing can be more different than their present situations and behaveour, And I hope you wont do yourself the wrong, nor give me Mortification as not to give him a good reception, and make himself sensible that you have forgiven him, which I should think should cost you very little, since there is no question of his staying with you, or of your trusting and employing him.

*   *   *   *

Adieu God Almighty bless you my D^rst Child whom I tenderly embrace and am all yours,   JAMES R.

[In spite of this appeal from his father, the Prince, two months later, not only refused to see Lord George Murray who had gone to Paris expressly to pay his respects, but sent to request Lord George to leave Paris, which he did.][2]

---

[1] From the Stuart Papers in Her Majesty's possession at Windsor, by permission. This letter is printed in the appendix to Browne's *History*, where there are several others on the same subject, showing the Old Chevalier's conciliatory disposition.

[2] Letter from L.G.M. to the Old Chevalier in the Stuart Papers, Browne's *History*, app. civ, cv.

ADDITIONAL NOTES

ADDITIONAL NOTE 1

MOVEMENTS OF THE 'DOUTELLE'

There is a certain mystery about the Prince's movements between July 25th and August 4th which has never been solved. Æneas MacDonald says that the party after the 26th coasted about the isles between Skye and Mull (i. 290). MacLeod of MacLeod, writing to the Lord President, mentions a ship hovering on parts of the coast between Ardnamurchan and Glenelg (C.P. 203); an informer's letter to Cope of August 3rd gives similar news (G.C.T. 116), and the *London Gazette* August 17th is quoted by Æneas MacDonald, though rather inconsequently, as corroborating his statement.

Mr. Henry Jenner has drawn my attention to a pamphlet in the British Museum entitled 'A Journal of the Pretender's Expedition to North Britain. Containing an Exact Narrative of his Transactions from the time of his Embarkation in France ; including several curious Particulars not hitherto made Public. Now publish'd from a manuscript wrote by an officer that accompanied him, which was found amongst his Papers since his Death occasioned by the two wounds he received at the Battle near Haddington.' (J. Collyer, London.)

It is a marvellous composition, written in the form of a daily journal, with all the gravity and veracity of Lemuel Gulliver or Robinson Crusoe.

It gives the most circumstantial accounts of the Prince's landing in Skye, Mull, and other places on the coast. Its statements are wildly impossible and the print is only one of what Patullo calls 'the injudicious, lying, catchpenny pamphlets,' of which many were written at the time under such titles as 'Ascanius,' 'The Young Adventurer,' 'The Wanderer,' and so forth ; it shows, however, that there were certain rumours afloat at the time, of the Prince's visiting the islands and harbours of the west coast, which may or may not have been founded on fact, and which formed the foundation of this romantic pamphlet of fifty-six pages.

ADDITIONAL NOTE 2

FRENCH, SPANISH, AND ENGLISH ASSISTANCE

THE history of the expected French and Spanish support has still to be written. Sheridan undertook the Prince's foreign correspondence, and his papers have still to be edited. John Murray's papers throw little light on this part of the expedition. That the Jacobites were bitterly disappointed is everywhere evident. Lord MacLeod goes the length of saying that the French did not desire the Prince's success, preferring 'at all times to have a pretender to the Crown of Great Britain' (L.M.N. 384); and the Prince himself endorses this view in his farewell letter from Borradale (April 25-28), in which he says: 'it is thought to be a politick [policy] though a false one of the French Court not to restore our master, but to keep a continual civil war in this country, which renders the English Government less powerful and of consequence themselves more.'

The actual succour given by the French, whatever their intentions may have been, was confined to the landing of about 1000 or 1200 men and some artillery and military stores. The total pecuniary assistance, says Æneas MacDonald, did not exceed £15,000 (State Papers Domestic: Examination of Æneas MacDonald, Jan. 12, 1747/8). Other sums received were the Chevalier's own or subscriptions from private sources.[1] Negative assistance was given, by the pressure put by France on the Dutch to withdraw their troops, by a threatened invasion, and by permitting ships to bring off fugitives after Culloden. The Spanish assistance[2] was confined to the occasional landing of privateers with money and stores, chronicled in the newspapers of the day, and a few officers, most of whom were captured with the *Hazard*. That some, at least, of the French Ministers felt they had neglected an opportunity is evident from the newspapers of the time. In the political summary of foreign news in the *Scots Magazine* of March, 1746, appears the following:—

'In a conference held at Versailles, in presence of the King, after his arrival, it is said Card. Tencin could not forbear discovering unusual warmth, and showing great dissatisfaction that the troops which were intended for Scotland were not gone, without waiting, as they had done, for the Spanish squadron. He said that, for want of these succours, the pretender's affairs had been much prejudiced, and would be irreparable, if the expedition was any longer delayed.'

In a so-called speech of the Duke of Perth at a council of war at Brampton, published in the *Edinburgh Evening Courant*, Jan. 7, 1746, printed below, the discontent and disappointment with the supineness

---

[1] MacDonald, the spy, mentioned at p. 103, who went on board the *Prince of Conti* at Lochnanuagh states that he heard the captain say 'that the French gold that had come over to Scotland in spring was collected by one Butler, an Irish priest, among the popish churches abroad.'—State Papers.

[2] Sir James Stewart received letters for the Prince from the Spanish Ambassador in Flanders and the Duc de Bouillon, containing distinct promises from the Kings of Spain and France of arms, money, and troops (B.H. Stuart Papers, App. ix.). These letters, which are dated August 1st, seem to have been printed and circulated. Translations are printed in III. 142, G.C.T. 189-90, C.P. 205-6. In G.C.T. they are said to have been brought over by one Arbuthnot who took them to Perth. These are no doubt the 'positive assurances' referred to on September 24th (*ante*, p. 18).

of the French Government and the English Jacobites is freely and pathetically expressed. This speech is almost certainly not genuine,[1] but it undoubtedly expresses the feelings of thoughtful Scots Jacobites.

THE DUKE OF PERTH'S SPEECH, at a GENERAL COUNCIL OF WAR, held at Brampton, near Carlisle, in Presence of the Pretender's eldest Son.

MAY IT PLEASE YOUR ROYAL HIGHNESS,—I Cannot help expressing the Concern I am in, to see so little Unanimity, and so much Heat and Animosity prevail in this Honourable Assembly, but my Concern wants Words sufficient to express it, when I reflect, that there are so many Reasons to complain of our present Situation; that there are so many Circumstances daily occurring to perplex us in our Projects; to weaken our Strength, and discourage us in our Undertaking.

Our Disappointments are so many, that we can number them only by the Days that have elapsed, since our first Insurrection, and their Greatness to be measured only by the Danger into which we are now plunged.

Our Hopes, before your Highness's Arrival in Scotland, were raised to the highest Pitch; and could only be equalled by the Zeal which Subjects of all Ranks in that Kingdom express'd for his Majesty. We flattered ourselves, that your Highness would have appeared back'd by a numerous Army, well supplied with Arms, Money, and Ammunition; their Number, we were made to believe, would not be less than Ten Thousand Men; and those of the best Troops of France: These were solemnly promised us by Mr. K——y, when with us in Spring last, and were told they were ready in the Ports of France with Transports, and a Fleet sufficient to protect the Landing. But when the Time came, how were we disappointed! Your Royal Highness landed in the West with a Retinue scarce sufficient for a private Gentleman; however, this did not discourage your faithful Clans from joining you, being still flattered, that the promised Succours were at Hand, and would certainly arrive before there was any Occasion of coming to an Action.

The Numbers of the faithful Highlanders still increased, till they were strong enough to venture for the East. When I had the Honour of joining your Highness at Perth, I was then assured that the French were actually embarked, and waited only a fair Wind; and that a considerable Insurrection would presently appear in the North, and several other Parts of England: The Places of the several Risings were particularly mentioned; and we were made acquainted with the Names of many considerable Men in England, who had undertaken to appear openly in his Majesty's Interest.

We were assured, that his Most Christian Majesty would certainly detain the English Forces in Flanders, and would hinder the Dutch from sending any Troops to Great Britain, by openly declaring your R—— Father his Ally. But how have we been disappointed in every Article of

---

[1] Cf. H.P.J. I. 296.

these Promises! The long promised Succours are not to this Day embarked; the Brest Squadron, which we were made to believe was to conduct the Transports, has long since sailed; but whither, no Man knows; only we are certain, they could not be designed for this Kingdom otherways they have had both Time and frequent fair Winds, to have brought them long before now.

His Most Christian Majesty has been so far from declaring himself openly in Favour of his Majesty, that his Minister at the Hague peremptorily declared to the States, that his Master had no Hand in the *Don Quixote* Expedition, as he was pleased to term your Highness's Undertaking in Scotland. The Dutch were allowed, without Molestation, to send over Six Thousand of those very Forces which were made Prisoners by the French King's Arms: Troops which could be of no Use to the Dutch in their own Country, by the Capitulation with France: Troops, which his Majesty of France could hinder being made use of against us, by a simple Declaration, that your R—— Father was his Ally; yet this was thought risquing too much in Favour of a People who had ventured their All upon the Assurances, Promises, and Faith of the French King; and what makes this Disappointment sit the heavier upon us is, that we are sure, if the Dutch had not sent these very identical Troops, they would have been much embarrassed to have spared others, to perform their Engagements with the Elector of Hanover.

But the Promise of detaining the English Forces, was as ill performed as the other, tho' that solely depended upon his most Christian Majesty's General. They had it in their Power to have hindered every Man of them from returning to England; and either I am very ill informed, or they might have made most of them Prisoners, had the French General been as sanguine at the latter End of the Campaign, as at the Beginning of it. But they were allowed to embark at Williamstadt, without Interruption; and are now almost all landed in England, without the Loss of a Transport, tho' the Possession of Ostend enabled his Most Christian Majesty, had he been so inclined, to have annoyed them much.

As to our Hopes from England, they have been as delusive as French Promises. When we arrived at Edinburgh, and had the Fortune to defeat Sir John Cope, our Assurances of a speedy Insurrection in England were renewed, the Days were fixed;[1] but these and many others have passed by, and not the least Appearance of any such Design; tho' on the Faith of them we continued unactive at Edinburgh. We might have proceeded Southward, while the Pannick of Cope's Defeat was fresh upon People's Minds, and before the Elector's Forces could possibly be got together; but that Opportunity was lost, in hopes, Sir, that your English Friends would declare for you, and supercede the Necessity of your loyal Clans going out of their own Country: But instead of any such Numbers declaring for you, we were entertained with nothing but Associations in

[1] Cf. Editorial Note, C.J., pp. 72, 73; also the Old Chevalier's opinion in a letter to his son Henry, Feb. 1746 (B.H. Stuart Papers, App. xxvi.).

all the Parts of England, in Defence of the Elector's Right; and not a
Man from that Kingdom, either joined us in Scotland, or made any Interest
to promote an Insurrection in your Favour, in their own Country.

At last, Sir, the Scene was shifted ; and new Conditions annexed to old
Promises : We were now told, that the French Embarkation was delayed,
until all the English Forces were drawn Northward ; and that then an
Invasion would be made on some Part of the South, now supposed to be
left destitute of Troops to defend them ; and that the English in the
North are now intimidated from rising, by the Vicinity of the Enemies
Troops ; but promise faithfully to join us, so soon as our Army sets Foot
on English Ground.   The general Disposition of the People is represented
to us, as strongly in our Interest ; and we are assured, that the Gates of
all Towns will almost open of themselves to receive us, and that the
People ardently wish to join us.

Notwithstanding the numerous Disappointments we met with, from the
first Beginning of this Affair ; yet we were again persuaded to listen to
delusive Promises.   We march from Edinburgh, enter England ; but
instead of that Disposition to join us, which we were flatter'd with, we find
those, who cannot oppose us, fly us, and those who have the least Shelter
from our Resentment, despise us, and treat us with the utmost Contempt.

We were assured by a Gentleman, upon whose Veracity I always thought
I might depend, and who now hears me, that the City of Carlisle we
have just now passed, would open its Gates to us at our first Appearance,
nay, that your Highness would have received the Keys of the City, some
Miles from the Place.   But how we were disappointed, you all know,
and with how much Contempt your Highness's Summons was treated.

The Value of the Place, I know to be insignificant ; nor do I believe
the Possession of it would be of any real Service to the main Cause ; yet
the Repulse we have met with from that paultry Town, has this Influence
upon me, to convince me, and I am afraid too late, that we are all made
the Tools of France, a Nation, whose Faith, like that of Carthage, is
become a Proverb ; and there is as little Dependence on the Promises of
English Malcontents, whose Zeal for your Royal House, these fifty Years
past, has manifested itself in nothing else, but Womanish Railing, vain
Boasting, and noisy Gasconades ; their Affection for you is most elevated
when in their Cups ; and their Sense of Loyalty only conspicuous in the
Absence of their Reason : Warmed with Wine, and a Tavern Fire, they
are Champions in your Cause ; but when cool, their Courage and Zeal,
Sir, for you and yours, evaporate with the Fumes of the Wine.

Thus, Sir, I conclude that we have no Dependance on English Assist-
ance ; to what Purpose proceed we any farther then ?   The Elector's
Forces are by far superior to ours in Number, daily supplied with Money,
Arms, Carriages and Ammunition ; while we were destitute of all these.
Your loyal Highlanders will fight for you with as much Zeal and Courage
as Men can boast of ; but shall we lead these brave Men to certain
Destruction ?   Were the Enemy's Number but equal to us, or but ex-

ceeded us in a small Proportion, I doubt not, but from the Justness of
our Cause, and the Courage of our Men, we might hope for Success ; but
when they are three to one, and that we must expect to diminish, rather
than increase, I should think myself guilty of the grossest Barbarity,
should I give my Voice to proceed any farther into England, until such of
this Nation as have promised to declare for the Cause, actually join us.

I entered, Sir, into this Affair, with as much Chearfulness as any Man
here ; I have contributed as much to support it as any; and I think, I
may say without Offence, that I have as much to lose by the Event as
most Men, and as little to hope. I shall venture my Life, with Pleasure,
to promote his Majesty's Interest ; yet, I think I owe something to the
Safety of these People who have followed my Fortune : I think I am
bound in Duty to prevent their Ruin, as much as in my Power, which I
think inevitable, if they proceed further ; therefore, I propose that we
return to Carlisle, and attempt to possess that City ; the taking of it may
give some Reputation to our Arms, and encourage the English to join us,
if they have any such Intention : If they have not, we must then make the
best Retreat back to the Highlands, while we can ; there disperse our unhappy Followers, and shift for ourselves in some Foreign Country, where
there is more Faith than in either France or England.

ADDITIONAL NOTE 3

DUTCH AND HESSIAN TROOPS

THE Dutch troops frequently mentioned in this narrative were a body
of 6000 men which the States-General had bound themselves by a treaty
(Jan. 30, 1713) to embark at the first call for the defence of his Britannic
Majesty and his crown.   The troops actually sent were parts of the
garrisons of Tournay and Dendermond, which had surrendered to the
French on June 20th (N.S.) 1745, and had been released under pledge
not to serve against the French King or his allies before Jan. 1747 (S. M.
294).   The greater part landed in the Thames under Count Maurice of
Nassau, Sept. 17th, and some others at Berwick and Newcastle (L. G.
Sept. 17-28), and formed part of Wade's army.   The French Government
remonstrated strongly against their employment on this service, and
put such pressure on Holland that the troops had to be withdrawn.   A
body of Hessians, under the Prince of Hesse, was substituted for the
Dutch, who returned, in the end of March, in the same ships that brought
over the Hessians (L. G. Mar. 1-4).   These Hessians, who landed at Leith
on February 8th, were a body of 6000, formerly on the French side,
which had capitulated to the Austrians in Bavaria, in April 1745, and, in
July, were taken into the pay of King George II.   'Between 4000 and
5000, among whom were some Hussars,' actually landed (S.M. 89).
For a contemporary abstract of these events, see *Scots Magazine*, 1745,
pp. 192, 294, 339, 382, and 1746, pp. 3, 137, and *passim* for the negotiations between the French and the States-General.

ADDITIONAL NOTE 4

THE RETREAT FROM DERBY

THE reasons for turning at Derby have often been discussed, but they seem simple enough, as explained by the comparatively recently published narrative of Lord MacLeod. MacLachlan had been sent from Carlisle to order up the reinforcements. A despatch in reply was received at Derby from Lord John Drummond, who refused to comply with the Prince's order, because, being in command of French troops, he had orders from King Louis not to advance until the Scots fortresses were reduced, or to do anything rash[1] (L.M.N. 385). The Jacobite leaders felt it absurd to advance on London with two armies on their flanks and rear, each far larger than their own, and a third army assembling at London to oppose them. If their Prince were killed or taken prisoner they would be the laughing-stock of Europe and their adventure stamped a *Don Quixote expedition*, a constantly recurring phrase in the correspondence of the time. Disappointed of any rising in England or invasion from France, and apparently misled by Drummond's representing his force and expectations to be greater than they really were, the Jacobite leaders thought it best to retire to their reinforcements and continue the campaign in Scotland. The Prince's army was less than five thousand irregular troops, while the enemy in their neighbourhood mustered more than treble that number of regulars, and the militia was being everywhere called out.—Cf. L.G.M. 54, C.J. 50, L.M.N. 385, M.K. 73, 87, H.H. 337, 339, etc., etc.

ADDITIONAL NOTE 5

TROOPS ENGAGED

AT the opening of hostilities, the troops then in Scotland were quartered thus: *Gardiner's Dragoons* (13th H.), at Stirling, Linlithgow, Musselburgh, Kelso, and Coldstream ; *Hamilton's Dragoons* (14th H.), at Haddington, Dunse, and adjacent places ; horses of both regiments at grass ; *Guise's* Regiment (6th of Foot), at Aberdeen and out-stations ; five companies of *Lee's* (44th), at Dumfries, Stranraer, Glasgow, and Stirling ; *Murray's* (46th), in the Highland barracks ; *Lascelles's* (47th), at Edinburgh and Leith ; two additional companies of the *Royal Scots* (1st), at Perth ; two of the *Scots Fusiliers* (21st), at Glasgow ; two of *Sempill's* (25th), at

---

[1] In the French King's Instructions to Lord John Drummond, printed from the Stuart Papers in Appendix to Browne's *History*, there is no order of this kind ; on the contrary, the instructions run thus : 'Il n'aura rien de plus pressé que de donner avis de son arrivée au Prince Edouard et de luy faire sçavoir que les secours qu'il luy amène est entièrement à ses ordres auxquels il se conformera en tout soit pour aller joindre son armée, ou pour agir séparément selon ses vues.'

Cupar-Fife ; three of Lord *John Murray's* Highlanders (42nd) at Crieff ; Lord *Loudon's* Highland Regiment was beginning to be raised, There were standing garrisons of Invalids in the castles (G.C.T. 5). There were no gunners (*ib.* 7).

BATTLE OF PRESTONPANS

SIR JOHN COPE'S ARMY

Exclusive of officers, sergeants, drums, etc.

	Rank and File.
3 Squadrons Gardiner's Dragoon's (13th H.) . . . }	567
3 ,, Hamilton's ,, (14th H.) . . }	
5 Companies Lee's Regiment (44th)	291
Murray's Regiment (46th)	580
8 companies Lascelles' Regiment (47th) . . . }	570
2 ,, Guise's ,, (6th) . . . }	
5 weak companies of Highlanders of Lord John Murray's Regiment (42nd), and Lord Loudon's Regiment .	183
Drummond's [Edinburgh] Volunteers	16
	2207
Add same proportion of officers, sergeants, drums, etc., as recorded at Culloden (16 per cent.) . . .	353
Total, ...	2560

6 Guns and some cohorns [mortars].

They had no gunners ; Lt.-Colonel Whiteford (Marines) served the guns with his own hands, and Mr. Griffith (Commissary) the cohorns.

The component parts of the army are taken from Cope's own statement at his trial (G.C.T. 38-43) and the numbers are filled in from the journals of the day (S.M. 441), with the exception of that of the volunteers, which is taken from Home's *History* (H.H. 106), the author of which was himself a volunteer. At his trial Cope stated that, his returns being lost, he could not determine the numbers with certainty, but he believed them to be about 600 Horse and 1400 Foot, besides a small number of Highlanders.

He also states that he had expected to be joined when marching north by the loyal clans of Highlanders, but with the exception of 200 Monroes who joined him at Inverness, and who refused to go to Dunbar, not a Highlander would go out with him. He complains that even the men of Lord John Murray's Regiment (42nd), who started with him from Stirling, had mouldered away on the march. He brought, however, from Inverness three companies of Lord Loudon's newly formed regiment, and two com panies of Guise's from Aberdeen.—(G.C.T. 5, 14, 27, 36, 143, etc. Cf. also II. 83-85 ; III. 7, etc. ; and the *Chiefs of Grant*, II. 149.)

THE PRINCE'S ARMY.

Patullo, the Prince's muster master (H.H. 331), estimates the army at about 2500, and this is roughly corroborated by the figures in the foregoing pages.

Augt. 19.	Clanranald, ...	200
	Lochiel, ...	700
	Keppoch, ...	300
26.	Stewart of Appin, ...	260
27.	Glengarry, ...	400
	Glencoe, ...	120
Sept. 4-10.	Robertson of Struan, . . .	200 [1]
11.	Duke of Perth, ...	150
18.	MacLachlans, ...	150
	Lord Nairne, ...	250 [2]
20.	Grants of Glenmoriston, . . .	100
	Cavalry, ...	50 [3]

2880

Less dismissed by Lochiel Augt. 30, . . . 150

2730

Allowance for desertion of Keppoch's men (Aug. 27), and a further allowance for leakage owing to desertion, illness, guards, etc., less a few men recruited in Edinburgh, ... 150

Total, . 2580

James More MacGregor or Drummond, not a very reliable authority,

---

[1] See p. 12, *n 2, ante.*

[2] Scott (*Tales of a Grandfather*, lxxviii.) estimates Lord Nairne's reinforcement at 1000 men including the MacLachlans. The only apparent authority I can find for this is a letter from the Duke of Atholl to Lord George Murray (Sept. 16), mentioning that he had been to Dunblane with Lord Nairne and 1000 men he was taking to the Prince (A.C. 19). Lord George in a later letter expresses his chagrin that the Atholl men who had arrived were so many fewer than expected, and that many had deserted (A.C. 25). Home, who actually fought on the Government side, and who certainly would not desire to minimise the Jacobite army, states that the number was only 250 (H.H. 331 *n*). Sir Walter also credits the Prince with a regiment of Lord George Murray, 350, and Menzies of Shian, 300, for which I can find no authority; they are not shown on Home's map, which figures only the forces tabulated here, with the addition of a body of MacGregors, but omitting the Glenmoriston Grants, who in another map are shown brigaded with Glengarry. It seems possible that Scott may have confused Lord Nairne's reinforcement with that which joined from Atholl at the end of October (cf. H.H. 137).

[3] These seem to have been country gentlemen and their servants who joined the army on the march.

in a letter to the Prince (D.M.L. 290), from Paris in 1753, states that he commanded a corps of his own at Prestonpans, and that 'he joyned no corps with his men.' The official Jacobite report of the battle mentions 'one body of the MacGregors with Glencairneg, and the rest of the MacGregors with the Duke of Perth's men under Major James Drummond' (S.M. 439). Only one body of MacGregors is figured in Home's plan of the battle, that in Perth's battalion, but it is evident there must have been two. MacPharic states that in the night march to the Netherbow of Edinburgh, the MacGregors joined Ardshiel's Stewarts, who only turned out 70 men for this service, while there were 200 MacGregors, but in the face of other records this must be received with reserve (N.S. 702).

The following is from John Murray of Broughton's Papers : ' He was reinforced [after leaving the Highlands] by a body of men from Atholl, 2 companies of MacGregors, 3 companies of the Duke of Perth's, some few of Struan Robertsons, with some volunteers from the lower parts of Perthshire, Stirlingshire, and Edinburgh.' These are probably all included in the forces mentioned above as joining under Struan, Perth, and Nairne, though possibly not enumerated with absolute accuracy in detail.

The *Caledonian Mercury*, 25th September, has the following : ' After the most strict inquiries, it now most obviously appears that only 1456 of the Highland Army engaged and foiled that commanded by Mr. Cope.' This probably merely means that the reserve were not engaged.

To show how rapidly desertion acted on the Highland Army, Patullo mentions that at a review a few days after the battle there only appeared about 1400. Some had been killed and wounded, others had gone home with the spoil (H.H. 331).

THE MARCH TO ENGLAND [1]

Patullo, writing to Home from memory, states that the Prince's army at the beginning of the march was about 5000 Foot and 500 Horse (H.H. 332), but Maxwell of Kirkconnell, who was a lieutenant in the Life Guards, with the rank of Lieut.-Colonel,[2] gives the numbers as about 400 Horse and 4500 Foot (M.K. 59). The details are taken from his statements and Captain Stuart's (of Ogilvy's) Journal :—

---

[1] A detailed Government estimate of the Jacobite army copied into all the newspapers of the time (*e.g.* S.M. 535), but owing to its source, of little value, gives a total number of 300 horse and 7287 foot.

[2] See Browne's *History*, Stuart Papers, Appendix, No. xxxix.

Life Guards, Lord Elcho's troop,[1] 120
      ,,   Elphinstone's (afterwards Lord Balmerino) do.,[2]   40
Lord Kilmarnock's (formerly Strathallan's) Horse (called
    also the Horse Grenadiers, sometimes the Perthshire
    Horse), not more than   .   .   . 100
Lord Pitsligo's Horse, Aberdeenshire and Banffshire,   . 120
The Hussars, commanded by Baggot, a French-Irish officer,
    of which Murray of Broughton was titular colonel,
    not more than   80

                   Total not more than   460

There were thirteen (afterwards fourteen) recognised regiments of Foot :—

> The Atholl Brigade, three battalions, under
>   Lord Nairne,
>   Mercer of Aldie,
>   Menzies of Shian,
>
> Lord Ogilvy's Regiment,
> Duke of Perth's,
> Gordon of Glenbucket's,
> John Roy Stewart's,
> (and subsequently) Townley's Manchester Regiment.

The Clan Regiments

Cameron of Lochiel.
MacDonald of Clanranald.
      ,,   ,, Glengarry.
      ,,   ,, Keppoch.
MacPherson of Cluny.
Stewart of Appin.

I have been unable to trace how the smaller bodies were brigaded, except that the Glenmoristons formed part of Glengarry's battalion (H.P.J. II. 413). The artillery consisted of 13 pieces, 2 to 4 pounders, six pieces landed from France (which Stuart occasionally called ' Swedish '), and seven pieces taken at Prestonpans (M.K. 51, 64).

---

[1] This does not exactly tally either with Murray's figures, p. 21, *n* 4, or with Maxwell's own total. The discrepancy is partly explained, however, by Kirkconnell's statement that Elcho's troop consisted of 5 officers, 62 gentlemen, and the rest servants.

[2] In Stuart's *Itinerary* (S.C.M.) this troop is frequently called ' Kenmure's.' Cf. *ante*, p. 21.

THE RETREAT FROM DERBY

THE PRINCE'S FORCE is estimated by Lord George Murray as 'not above 5000 men, if so many,' which corroborates Kirkconnell's enumeration. A garrison had been left at Carlisle, but this had more than been compensated for by the Manchester Regiment. There was practically no desertion in England.

THE DUKE OF CUMBERLAND'S ARMY

This force of five regiments of cavalry and eleven battalions of infantry is detailed by Lieutenant Archibald Campbell, A.D.C. to General Bland, from a general order of Cumberland's of Dec. 4 (D.C. 248):—

Bland's Dragoons (3rd H.).	Ligonier's Horse (7th D.G.).[1]
Lord Mark Kerr's Dragoons (11th H.).	Cobham's Dragoons (10th H.).

Kingston's Horse (since disbanded).

3 Battalions of Footguards.	Howard's (3rd).[2]
Sempill's (25th).	Skelton's (12th).
Campbell's (21st).	Sowles's (11th).
Johnson's (33rd).	Handasyde's (31st).
Douglas's (32nd).	

In the train there were 30 pieces of cannon, 6 to 4 pounders (S.M. 535).

The Duke of Bedford's newly raised regiment was also at Tamworth (L.G. Nov. 30-Dec. 3), and Bligh's (20th) joined the Duke shortly afterwards and marched in the pursuit to Carlisle (D.C. 254, R.H.). These troops represented a force of probably not less than 7000 foot and 1500 horse.

MARSHAL WADE'S ARMY

It is somewhat difficult to estimate Wade's force, owing to the meagre information given in the newspapers, and the non-existence of many regimental histories. It originally assembled at Doncaster, and marched to Newcastle, where it was reinforced by troops landed direct from Holland in the Tyne and at Berwick, as well as troops from Ireland, and the cavalry that had fled from Prestonpans. It afterwards marched to Wetherby and Doncaster, and again returned to the north. The

---

[1] One squadron of Ligonier's was in London, see p. 96, *post*.

[2] Part (at least) of this regiment landed in the Tyne and joined Wade (L.G. Oct. 22-26). Part also landed in the Thames (L.G. Sept. 21-24) and joined Cumberland (D.C. 248). The official regimental history only mentions Wade's army. I cannot discover whether there were two battalions of the regiment, or only different detachments of the same battalion. There was another 'Howard's' regiment (19th), but it remained in the Netherlands (R.H.).

following computation is made from the newspapers of the day, checked and supplemented from official histories of the regiments:—

Montague's (or the Queen's) Horse (2 D.G.).
Wade's Horse (3 D.G.).
St. George's Dragoons (8th H.).
Francis Ligonier's (late Gardiner's) Dragoons (13th H.).
Hamilton's Dragoons (14th H.).
Oglethorpe's Georgian Rangers.[1]
The Royal Hunters.[2]

2nd Battalion St. Clair's (1st).	Price's (14th).
Howard's (3rd).	Blakeney's (27th).
Barrel's (4th).	Cholmondeley's (34th).
Wolfe's (8th).	Fleming's (36th).
Pulteney's (13th).	Ligonier's (48th).
Battereau's (since disbanded).	

The Dutch troops, about 6000.

Of these infantry regiments most of the Dutch (L.G. Sept. 17-21) as well as Pulteney's and Cholmondeley's came from Flanders, viâ the Thames (L.G. Sept. 21-24): St. Clair's (R.H.) and Battereau's (E.E.C. Nov. 11) came from Ireland, seven battalions and some Dutch came direct from Holland to Berwick and the Tyne with Albemarle (L.G. Oct. 22-29).

The newspapers of the day estimate Wade's army at 14,000 foot and 4,000 horse (E.E.C. Nov. 4); but that may be an exaggeration, or it may include some other regiments whose official histories have not been published, or possibly militia and yeomanry whose movements I have been unable to discover. Price's and Ligonier's Foot were sent along with Ligonier's and Hamilton's Dragoons to Edinburgh on the 14th November under General Handasyde (S.M. 538). But I have not been able to trace how much of the force made the abortive march towards Carlisle, nor how much marched towards Derby. On the Prince's retreat from Derby, all Wade's cavalry, except the two regiments sent to Edinburgh in November, were sent under Oglethorpe to assist Cumberland in the pursuit. They joined at Preston on December 13th (L.G., Dec. 14-17).

Cumberland pursued the Prince with all his cavalry and mounted infantry.[3] About 1000 infantry were employed from Sowles's, Skelton's,

---

[1] The Rangers were a regiment recruited by General Oglethorpe for service in Georgia, of which colony he was founder. When on the point of sailing for America their course was diverted to Hull, whence they joined Wade at Newcastle.—Wright's *Memoir of Oglethorpe*, p. 358.

[2] The Royal Hunters seem to have been a corps of Yorkshire volunteers (S.M. 489). Their regimental song set to music is printed in the *Gentleman's Magazine*, Dec. 1745, p. 664.

[3] L.G. Dec. 7-14. Chevalier Johnstone states that the infantry were mounted behind the dragoons (C.J. 68), but in Chancellor Ferguson's paper, p. 193 (see p. 32, n 1, *ante*), it is stated that horses for the infantry were supplied by the neighbouring gentry.

and Bligh's (R.H.).   They were joined by a regiment of Liverpool militia,
which assisted at the siege of Carlisle.

THE ARMY AT FINCHLEY COMMON

This gathering, rendered famous by Hogarth's picture, is not referred
to in the *London Gazette*.   In contemporary journals the following
paragraphs appear :—

'We hear that there is to be a camp on Finchley Common in a few days, under
the command of the Earl of Stair.'—*General Evening Post*, Dec. 3-5.

'It being apprehended that the rebels were coming forward from Derby for
London, and that the Duke would not be able to come up with them, it was
resolved to form a camp on Finchley common ; for which purpose the guard, Ld.
John Murray's (the old highland) regiment, etc., marched on the 7th to Highgate,
Enfield, and Barnet ; and a large train of artillery was sent from the tower.   The
same day, the lieutenancy of London directed, that two regiments of the trained
bands should be out every night, and one in the daytime.   But upon the news of
the rebels retreat, the orders given the troops were countermanded.'—*Scots
Magazine*, p. 582.

10th Dec.   'The Guards and other regiments sent on 7th to Highgate, Enfield,
and Barnet in order to form a camp at Finchley Common were countermanded.

14th Dec.   Marched through London for Kent and Sussex to oppose any landing
of the French there, the Royal Irish, Scotch, and Welch Fusileers, a squadron
of Ligonier's Horse, Hawtrey's and Rich's Dragoons.'—*Gentleman's Magazine*,
pp. 665, 666.

BATTLE OF FALKIRK

THE PRINCE'S ARMY

The Prince's army was largely recruited at Bannockburn.   Patullo
states that at a review held at Glasgow there were 'full 5000' present.
At Falkirk he estimates the troops at 8000, in addition to about 1000
(Forbes says 1200) left to besiege Stirling Castle (H.H. 332).

The battalions shown on Home's map of the battle are :—

Keppoch.	Athole, 3 battalions.
Clanranald.	Ogilvy, 2 battalions.
Glengarry.	Lord Lewis Gordon, 2 battalions.
Farquharson.	Lord John Drummond, 2 battalions.
Lord Cromarty.	The MacLachlans are mentioned but not figured,
MacIntosh.	and in another map are shown brigaded with
MacPherson.	Drummond's.
Fraser.	The Cavalry are not figured, but their presence is
Lochiel.	mentioned, and they are shown in other maps.
Appin.	

Cobham's Dragoons (10th H.),	Price's (14th).
Ligonier's Dragoons (13th H.),	Ligonier's (48th).
Hamilton's Dragoons (14th H.)	Blakeney's (27th).
	Monro's (37th).
Wolfe's (8th).	Fleming's (36th).
Cholmondeley's (34th).	Barrel's (4th).
Pultenzy's (13th).	Battereau's (disbanded).
St. Clair's (1st).	Howard's (3rd).

The official return (H.H. 392) gives the numbers under Hawley, on Jan. 13th, as 5488 infantry and 519 dragoons. These numbers should be augmented by 16 per cent. for officers, sergeants, drummers, etc., —the proportion recorded for Culloden (say 960)—making a total of 6967, and to this number must be added Cobham's Dragoons, who did not join him until the 15th, also the Glasgow Militia and the Argyleshire Highlanders (S.M. 40).

BATTLE OF CULLODEN
THE PRINCE'S ARMY

Patullo states that the number on the rolls was 8000, but that owing to absentees on other expeditions, and men exhausted by the night march to Nairn, it was not possible to bring 5000 to the field (H.H. 332).

The principal absentees were : Lord Cromarty, with a large force in Sutherland ; Barrisdale, Glengyle, and MacKinnon ; Cluny MacPherson had not returned from Badenoch (II. 275, L.G.M. 120, etc.).

Sir Robert Strange states that over 1000 men were lying asleep in the Culloden parks unconscious of the battle (M.S.L. I. 60).

The map and numbers in the *Scots Magazine*, p. 217, are quite untrustworthy. Finlayson's Map of Culloden, the most detailed, and, probably, the most accurate plan of the battle, shows the following forces on the field :—

First Line.	Second Line.
Atholl.	Highland Horse.
Camerons.	[probably all the Scottish Cavalry
Stewarts of Appin.	remaining.]
John Roy Stewart.	Bannerman of Elsick.
Frasers.	Glenbucket.
MacIntoshes.	[French] Royal Scots.
Farquharsons.	Kilmarnock.
MacLeans [and MacLachlans].	[French] Irish Picquets.
MacLeods.	Lord Lewis Gordon.
Chisholms.[1]	Fitzjames Horse.
Clanranald.	
Keppoch.	*Third Line.*
Glengarry.	Lord Ogilvy's Battalions
Duke of Perth.	in Reserve.

---

[1] I have been unable to discover when and where the Chisholms joined the

THE DUKE OF CUMBERLAND'S ARMY

Cobham's Dragoons (10th H.).   Lord Mark Kerr's Dragoons (11th H.).
Kingston's Horse (disbanded).

Royal Scots, St. Clair's (1st).	Blakeney's (27th).
Howard's (3rd).	Cholmondeley (34th).
Barrel's (4th).	Fleming's (36th).
Wolfe's (8th).	Dejean's, formerly Munro's (37th).
Pulteney's (13th).	Conway's, formerly Ligonier's (48th).
Price's (14th).	Battereau's (disbanded).
Bligh's (20th).	
Campbell's (21st).	Lord Loudon's Regiment.
Sempill's (25th).	Argyleshire Militia.

The numbers given out at the time (S.M. 216), and accepted as correct
in Regimental Histories, are :

Regular Infantry (15 Regiments) Rank and File, . .	5521
,, ,, Officers, Sergeants, and Drummers, .	890
Cavalry, Loudon's and Argyleshire men, . . .	2400
Total, . .	8811

ADDITIONAL NOTE 6

NEIL MacEACHAIN'S[1] NARRATIVE

IN the *New Monthly Magazine* for 1840 there is a narrative, the manuscript of which, the editor states, was purchased some twenty years before
along with miniatures of Prince Charles and his brother Henry from a
hairdresser in France, who was believed to be the son of Neil MacEachain
or MacDonald. This could not have been. Marshal MacDonald was
his only son who survived infancy. At Neil's death, the son being
with his regiment, the father's effects were consigned to the care of
MacNab, a brother exile, who was imprisoned during the Revolution, and
all Neil's papers were irretrievably lost. But from whatever source the
manuscript came into the editor's hands, there can be no doubt of its
genuineness, and that it could only have been written by Neil himself.
The internal evidence is perfect ; it carries conviction in every line. It
is the missing link which fits into and supplements, with entire completeness, the stories preserved by Bishop Forbes.

Prince. In L.P.R. 72, the 'particulars of facts' mentioned are that Roderick
Chisholm, fourth son of the Chief, was at Culloden, and there killed, with thirty
men out of his company of eighty.

[1] In *The Lyon* the name is generally spelt MacKechan.

It is a mistake to suppose that Neil MacEachain was a servant or even retainer of Flora MacDonald's in the usual sense of the term. The MacEachains (sons of Hector) were a branch of the Clanranald family. Neil, who was born in 1719,[1] had been educated in France for the priesthood, but had not taken orders (I. 80). Returning to South Uist he became parish schoolmaster, and was acting as tutor in Clanranald's family when Lady Clanranald or Hugh of Armadale selected him as the Prince's companion on account of his knowledge of French and other languages (I. 80, II. 46, C.R.C. App. A. 460).

That Neil MacEachain was known to be capable of using his pen is shown by Kingsburgh's suggestion that he had written *Alexis,* which is an account of the Prince's adventures up to his leaving Skye, written in the form of a pastoral allegory (I. 79). The *Narrative* is of very different style, but there are two incidents common to both : both mention that in crossing to Skye the boat escaped from a man-o'-war by mist, and both emphasise the Prince's awkwardness in managing his petticoats. MacEachain is not mentioned by O'Neil unless he is the ' little herd ' referred to at I. 372. Fortunately Edward Burke supplies the missing information, and tells us that Neil MacEachain (whom he calls Neil MacDonald) guided the Prince and O'Neil to Rossinish (I. 196). This ignoring of Neil was resented by Bishop Forbes himself on several occasions (*e.g.* I. 330, *n* 2, 373, *n* 2), and it is probable that this ' good-natured and very timorous ' young man (I. 80) was looked upon as a mere servant or message-lad, too insignificant to be mentioned at all, or it may be that his effacement was the result of jealousy because he was preferred to O'Neil as the Prince and Flora's companion to Skye.

In the *Narrative* MacEachain informs us that the Prince's host in the Braes of Morar near Meoble was Angus MacEachine [Borradale's son-in-law] ; that while waiting at Borradale the Prince had daily conferences with young Clanranald and Barrisdale ; that it was in spite of the remonstrances of these Highlanders and by the secret advice of O'Neil, O'Sullivan, and Allan MacDonald that the Prince determined to abandon Scotland and escape ; but he makes no mention of John Hay's presence at Borradale, and his story at this period is only hearsay.

But when the Prince reaches Benbecula, where the news of his arrival reached Clanranald at the moment that Neil and the Rev. John MacAulay were dining with him, his story becomes more valuable. He relates how MacAulay sent a spy to find out the Prince's intentions, and how he sent a messenger to the minister of Stornoway to apprise Seaforth's factor and have the Prince apprehended.

MacEachain's dates and details do not entirely correspond with Donald MacLeod's, which are followed in this Itinerary, but he gives some interesting sidelights. He describes the disguises assumed by the party before landing in Scalpa. He apparently does not like Donald

---

[1] *Recollections of Marshal MacDonald,* London, 1892.

Campbell, the Prince's faithful host in Scalpa, and calls him 'an enemy by name and a downright hypocrite in his heart.'[1] He believes O'Neil's story of Donald MacLeod's getting drunk[2] after arranging with the ship captain to charter a brig for the Orkneys, and revealing to him who the passengers were; but his story of the fruitless journey to Lewis, being only hearsay, is imperfect, though the salient incidents corroborate Donald MacLeod.

When he comes to attend the Prince as guide through South Uist his narrative teems with interest. He is as garrulous and minute about his hero as Boswell is about Johnson, and he tells us several things omitted in other narratives. He relates that O'Neil was sent to the Lewis to try and engage a ship for France, but being discovered he was obliged to return unsuccessful to the Prince, 'who did not care much for him ever after.'

He also informs us that Flora's expedition was the inception of her stepfather, Hugh MacDonald of Armadale, who was in South Uist in command of the militia, ostensibly to apprehend the Prince, not to help him. But the charm of the narrative is in the Boswellian touches, which nowhere else are to be found in such perfection. As a magazine article nearly sixty years old is not very accessible, a few quotations from it are given here.

He tells how, when prevented from entering Stornoway, the Prince was 'raging with anger and fear,' and that 'the mob made a dreadful noise about the house;' that, when in Euirn his followers declined to touch some salt fish that had been left by the fishermen:

'he himself, went in a passion, and carried half a dozen of them in his arms, and threw them in the boat, saying, since they were all so gentle and scroupelous, that he would take the sin upon himself, and show them the exemple.'

He repeats the Prince's own account of losing a horse at Culloden:

'for (says he) as I was riding up to the right wing, my horse began to kick, at which I was much surprised, being very quiet, and peaceable formerly, and looking narrowly to him to see what was the matter with him, I observed the blood gushing out of his side. Oh! oh! says I (speaking of the horse), if this be the story with you, you have no less than reason to be uneasie, whereupon I was oblidged to dismount and take another.'

He is impressed with the Prince's powers of eating and drinking:

'he had always a good appetite, and could eat any meat that came in his way, as well as those who was accustomed to it from their infancy. He took care to warm his stomach every morning with a hearty bumper of brandy, of which he always drank a vast deal; for he was seen to drink a whole bottle of a day without being in the least concerned.'

Here is his description of the morning after the carouse with Baleshair:

'Boystile came next day, and was received by the prince with open arms, and found

---

[1] Cf. Edward Burke: 'one of the best, honestest fellows that ever drew breath' (I. 191).

[2] Cf. I. 168, 277, 369

some of the gentlemen of the country who came to see him the day before, of whose number was Hugh Macdonald, of Ballissher, from Nort Wist, who was ready to sacrifice his life and fortune for the prince's safety, (I say) Boystile at his arrival found all these lying in their bed, very much disordered by the foregoing night's carouse, while his royal highness was the only one who was able to take care of the rest, in heaping them with plaids, and at the same time merrily sung the *De profundis* for the rest of their souls' (cf. II. 97).

He tells of O'Neil's admiration for Flora :

'Mr. O'Neil was obliged to go upon that expedition ; who was mighty well pleased to be intrusted with that embassy, not so much to further the prince's affairs, as to be in company with Miss Flora, for whom he professed a great deal of kindness at that time.'

He depicts the Prince in many moods :

'at other times he was so hearty and merry, that he danced for a whole hour together, having no other musick but some highland reel which he whistled away as he tripped along. It happened one day as he was walking along the coast with Neil and the rest of the gentlemen, being an excessive hot day, they spied a number of young whales approaching pretty near the shore, and observing them to make straight for the rock whereon they sat down, he sent immediately for his fusee, and as they came within his reach he fired at them ; and being informed some time before that Neil was an incomparable good swimmer, he ordered him to strip and hall ashore the whale, which he swore he had shot dead [not considering that that office was fitter for dogs rather than for men].[1] Neil, in obedience to his orders and to humour him, began to strip very slowly till he saw the whale which had received no hurt, out of sight.'

When, like David Balfour in *Kidnapped*, he is left by his boatmen on a tidal island, his consternation is most natural :

Neil 'observed an arm of the sea come in betwixt him and the rest of the land, which formed an island ; he returned immediately and informed the prince, who started up like a mad man and walked to the end of the island at such a rate as if he had a mind to fly over to the other side, but his career was soon stopped ; whereupon he fell a sculding Neil as if it had been his fault, and the cursed rascals (meaning the boatmen) who land'd them upon that desert island designedly that he might starve with hunger and cold, in short, there was no pacifying him, till, at last, Neil told him to comfort himself, that he would sweem over to the other side and would bring a boat in half an hour's time, from that moment he never gave Neil one minute's rest, till, to please him, he began to strip, notwithstanding that it rained most prodigiously.' [They subsequently crossed the loch dry-shod.]

Neil details what they had to eat and drink, or occasionally starve upon, at every halting-place. At the booman's house

the Prince 'desired Neil to ask the wife if she had any eatables. She said that she had nothing except a chapin of milk she kept for her bairns, which Neil desired her to warm in a pot, and when it was hot to froth it up with the machine made for that purpose. When all was ready, the wife placed the pot before the prince and Neil, and gave them two horn spoons as coarse as ever was made use of, the prince ask't Neil what it was, who told it was fresh creme, he not doubting but it was really so, and at the same time believing it to be solid, pushed his hand to the very

---

[1] Erased in manuscript.

wrist in the scalded milk, which made him draw back his hand in the greatest hurry, all full of wrath, and dropt his spoon in the pot. Neil had all the difficulty imaginable to keep his gravity, to hear him curse the wife and her pot a hundred times, calling her a vile witch, for (says he) she contrived it a purpose that we might burn ourselves. Neil, seeing him altogether out of humour, in order to pacify him, told him he would take a stick and labour her to an inch of her life with it, and immediately ran to an oar of the boat that was lying before him to knock out her brains. The prince, believing him to be serious, begged of him not to touch her.'

Here is his description of the scandal caused to the congregation returning from church (it was a Sunday), by Kingsburgh's attention to Miss MacDonald's waiting-maid :

'they continued to speak of the impudence and assurance of Miss Burk, who was not ashamed to walk and keep company with Kingsborough, and was no less vexed than surprised how he took so much notice of her, when he never minded her mistress who was so near at hand. . . . But what they most took notice of all was, when Kingsborough and his companion was come to a rivulet about knee deep which crossed the high rod, to see Burk take up her petty coats so high when she entred the water. The poor fellows were quite confounded at this last sight.'

The whole narrative, which is full of pawky humour, is one that would have delighted Bishop Forbes.

Neil's after career may be told in a few words. He accompanied the Prince to France (ii. 25), and joined Ogilvy's Scots regiment. He never saw his country again. The regiment was disbanded at the peace of 1763. Neil retired on a pension of thirty pounds to Sancerre, and married a penniless girl. He was gentle, she was quick-tempered ; he was naturally silent, she was a great talker ; two or three years before his death they voluntarily separated. Of four children, only the Marshal and one daughter survived infancy.

Neil was very studious, well versed in Greek and Latin, as well as in French, English, and Gaelic. His memory was well stored and full of anecdote. He was a good musician, playing the violin, and was much esteemed by the society of that time. He died in 1788.[1]

ADDITIONAL NOTE 7

THE SHIP IN WHICH THE PRINCE SAILED TO FRANCE

THERE is a minor mystery about the name of the ship that bore the Prince to France, which I have been unable to fathom. Colonel Warren, in a letter to O'Brien of 29th August N.S., says he is going to Scotland with *L'Heureux* and the *Prince of Conti* to try and bring off the Prince (Stuart Papers). Glenaladale says the ship that the Prince sailed in was

---

[1] *Recollections of Marshal MacDonald*, which also contains in vol. i. an appendix giving a brief account of the MacEachain family, by Mr. Alexander Carmichael.

the *Happy* (I. 351), Burton says it was the *Bellona* (I. 295), and on Finlayson's map it is also called the *Bellona*. In one passage in the *Scots
Magazine* it is said to be the *Happy* (S.M. 1746, p. 492), while in another
it is called the *Bellona* (S.M. 1749, p. 639). Warren, writing to the Old
Chevalier on October 10th N.S., the day of landing in Roscou, reports he
has brought back the Prince, but does not mention the name of the ship,
nor is it shown on Grante's map. Having the curiosity to probe the
problem, I examined some of the reports of Lord Albemarle's spies preserved in the Record Office, but the confusion only got worse. These
spies seem to have been, on the whole, exceedingly well informed, although
their reports convey the shrewd suspicion that the information was always
given too late to be of use. They all agree that two French ships arrived
in Lochnanuagh on the 6th. One spy, M'Hevoul, mentions that one of
them was the *Prince of Conti*, and in it the Prince went off; he does not
name the other. Another, Donald MacDonald, apparently the same man
who acted as interpreter to Bishop Forbes in 1751 (III. 90, 97), actually
went on board the *Prince of Conti*, and he states that the other ship was
named the *Louine*, which is possibly his misinterpretation of *L'Heureux*, as
heard rapidly pronounced; in this he is entirely corroborated by a third
spy, whose name is not given. Both state that two other French ships
were expected, but both informers had left before the Prince had arrived
at Borradale. A fourth spy, a ship captain of Campbeltown, reports that
there had been four French ships in Lochnanuagh, in one of which the
Prince sailed, but he does not name any of them.

In the declaration of one of these spies there is a quaint side-light
thrown on the state of the times. Donald MacDonald, though a native
of South Uist, was an Edinburgh tailor who numbered among his customers 'young Clanranald and other persons of distinction in Lochaber.'
He had gone 'in the way of his trade' to try to get his accounts paid.
Very naturally he met 'with little success,' though he was courteously
treated by young Clanranald, with whom he dined on board the *Prince
of Conti*. He actually managed to recover £12 from his customers, but
on his way back was accosted by 'three of the Camerons armed with
firearms, who laid hold of the declarant's money,' but after detaining
him three days they returned him £4 and let him go (State Papers
Domestic: Sep. 30, 1746).

ADDITIONAL NOTE 8

CONTEMPORARY MAPS

Two maps of the expedition are referred to in *The Lyon*, each of which
has an itinerary attached, and there is yet a third contemporary map
printed in Rome. All are so rare, and yet so interesting, that I venture
to give a somewhat detailed description of them.

COLONEL GRANTE'S MAP.

The first, mentioned by Forbes in vol. II. p. 377, is by Colonel J. A. Grante, a French officer of Scots origin, who was Master of Ordnance to the Prince, and who is several times referred to in these pages.

The French edition of Grante's map, of which there is a copy in the British Museum, is a large sheet, 61 inches high and 64 inches wide. The scale approximates to 10 miles to the inch—the scale of the map that accompanies this volume. It bears the following title :

'Carte où sont tracées toutes les différentes routes, que S.A.R. Charles
' Edward Prince de Galles a suivies dans la grand Bretagne, et les
' Marches, tant de son armée que de celle de l'Ennemi. On y trouve
' aussi les siéges qui ont été faits et les Batailles qui ont été données dans
' son entreprise.

'Cette Carte sera très utile pour l'Histoire, les dates des principaux
' événements y étant marqués avec exactitude. Dressée et présentée à
' Son Altesse Royale par son très humble et très obéissant Serviteur,
'J. A. GRANTE.'
And at the foot ' Avec privilége du Roy 1748.'

The map is beautifully engraved in the style of the day, ornamented with ships, tritons, cupids, and other allegorical figures. It is of no geographical value, but is a good military diagram. Grante himself thus explains it : ' On s'est plutôt attaché dans cette Carte à donner
' les routes et les mouvemens des armées qu'à faire une description géo-
' graphique : et l'on s'est servi d'une vieille Carte de Morden sans y rien
' changer, la grandeur et l'exactitude en ayant paru assez convenables au
' projet qu'on avoit formé.' Morden's chart, on which it is founded, is generally dated 1700. Grante's map shows the French coast of the English Channel and the whole of Great Britain and Ireland, chiefly in outline, until Scotland is reached, where diagrammatic and imaginary mountains are added. The routes of the Prince and his army, and those of the government troops, are shown in different linings, and military indications of the different sieges are added.

The Prince's route after Culloden is indicated in conventional sweeps, of no topographical value, but most graphically diagrammatising his dangers from the numerous hostile camps that he had to pass and avoid, which camps are sketched on the map.

The most interesting features are two tables engraved in blank spaces. One is headed ' Dates des événemens les plus considérables.' These dates are given in New Style, then used in France but not in Great Britain. When translated into Old Style they differ but little from the other authorities of events that occurred before Culloden. In chronicling the events, prominence is given, as befits an Ordnance officer, to the siege operations of the Expedition, and the details of the Prince's wanderings are not given. There is one notable discrepancy in the date of the landing at Borradale, which is given as July 26 N.S., that is July

15 O.S. This has evidently been caused by a confusion between Old Style and New Style.

Another date will be interesting to readers of *The Lyon*—that of the Prince's final departure (see *Lyon*, vol. ii. p. 377), which is chronicled as September 30 N.S., that is, September 19 in English style. Bishop Forbes had noted a discrepancy of one day here from the accepted date of September 20; but he makes the mistake of calling it one day after the 20th, instead of one day before.

Two passages in the tables are of especial interest. It may be safely assumed that they were dictated, or at least inspired, by the Prince himself, and they give his own version of his reasons for abandoning the struggle and his own description of the dangers encountered in his wanderings.

'ÉVÉNEMENS QUI ONT SUIVI LA BATAILLE DE CULLODEN. Après cette
' funeste bataille, le Prince s'étant rendu aux environs du lieu marqué
' pour le rendez-vous, proposa aux Chefs de rassembler les forces qui
' pouvoient lui rester; mais il reconnut que les mêmes difficultez, qui
' l'avoient auparavant empêché de se retirer dans les montagnes, sub-
' sistoient encore, et que l'impossibilité de trouver des vivres rendoit
' impraticable un pareil projet : alors la sûreté de sa personne devint un
' unique et commun objet; il ne lui restoit que la ressource de se mettre
' à couvert, jusqu'à ce qu'il se fût présenté quelque Vaisseau, qui le
' transportât au Continent.'

' Les petits camps qu'on a marquez sur les montagnes et dans les iles,
' désignent les différents postes pris par les gens de guerre qui cherchoient
' le Prince après la déroute de son armée. Il se trouva dans la dangereuse
' nécessité de s'exposer à traverser quelquefois deux, trois et quatre de
' ces camps dans un même jour, tantôt avançant, tantôt retournant sur
' ses pas, suivant que la prudence le lui dictoit, et qu'il couroit plus ou
' moins de risque par l'examen des sentinelles et des patrouilles et par la
' continuelle recherche des partis ennemis.

' Caché pendant le jour il profitoit des ténèbres de la nuit, pour
' avancer sa route toujours à pied et sous un habit à la mode des gens du
' pais, dont un ou deux l'accompagnoient, soit pour le guider dans
' l'obscurité soit pour aller le jour à la découverte, et s'instruire des
' mouvemens des troupes, qui changeoient à tous momens de situation,
' suivant qu'elles croyoient pouvoir le surprendre ou dans un vallon, ou
' sur une montagne, ou au passage d'un Lac et des bras de mer qui
' séparent les Isles, ou qui s'avancent dans les terres : ce que n'a pas
' heureusement permis la Providence, qui veilloit à la conservation d'un
' Prince aussi précieux.'

There is also an ENGLISH EDITION of this map. It is of much smaller scale, approximating 40 miles to the inch, and the sheet is $24\frac{1}{2}$ inches high by $15\frac{3}{4}$ inches wide to outside of printed border. The title runs thus:

'A Chart Wherein are mark'd all the different Routs of P. Edward i n
'Great Britain, and the Marches of his Army and the English. The
'Sieges are distinguish'd and the Battles that were Fought in this Enter-
'prise. This Chart (with the Book) will be very useful in History, the
'Dates of the principal Events being mark'd with the greatest care and
'exactness.'

A panel in one corner bears the dedication, 'Inscrib'd to all The
'Honest,' superscribed with the motto, 'Astræa redit.' The imprint
runs, 'Drawn by J. A. Grante, Colonel of the Artillery to the Pr. in
'Scotland. Engrav'd in Edinburgh. Sold in May's Buildings, Covent
'Garden. [Price 5s. with the Book.']

The map is a reduced copy of the French one, roughly and inaccu-
rately copied. The notes engraved on the French edition are not on the
Edinburgh chart, but are incorporated in a little book which bears this
title:

'A/Description/of a/chart/wherin are marked out/All the different
'Routes/of/Prince Edward/in/Great Britain/and/the Marches of his Army
'and the/E—gl—sh.

'The Sieges are distinguished and the Battles that were fought in his
'Enterprise. N.B.—This Book, and the Chart printed from off a copper
'plate will be very useful in History; the Dates of the principal events
'being marked with the greatest exactness. Edinburgh. Printed
'Sold in Mays Buildings. Covent Garden. MDCCXLIX.'

The size of page is 6¾ inches by 4 inches. The letterpress is a literal
translation of the tables engraved on the French map, but giving the Old
Style dates in addition to the New Style, which alone are shown on the
French map. It contains all the errors of its original. A copy of the
book and map is to be seen in the British Museum, and I have also to
thank Mr. Smail, a member of this Society, for the loan of a copy of the
map, which shows part of the imprint mutilated in the Museum copy, in
which it has been restored in handwriting.

THE ROMAN MAP.

This map is not in the British Museum, and the only copy I know of
is in possession of the Earl of Crawford at Haigh Hall, to whom, and
to Mr. J. P. Edmond, I am indebted for the loan of it. It bears this
title:

'Carte de la Grande Bretagne et d'Irlande où l'on voit tout le détail
'de l'entreprise de S.A.R. Charles Prince de Galles commencée MDCCXLV.
'Dédiée à sa Majesté Jaques III. Roi de la Grande Bretagne, &c.' It is
not dated, but bears the imprint 'Pietro e Ferdinando Campana sculp.
'in Roma. sup. per.'

The map appears to be a copy of Grante's, as it repeats all Grante's
information, though with slight textual variation, and shows the same area.
Though the scale is much smaller, approximating 27 miles to an inch, the

topography is better. The Prince's routes are shown as in Grante's. The map itself is 34¾ inches high and 28¼ inches wide to outside of printed borders; on each side wings are affixed, on one of which is given Grante's 'Abrégé des principales actions' in French, and on the other the same information translated into Italian and headed 'Compendio delle Azzioni,' etc. These tables are engraved in beautiful large script, and extend the whole height of the map. Within the border proper, Grante's other tables are engraved in French only.

JOHN FINLAYSON'S MAP

The hunting for John Finlayson's Map, for which Bishop Forbes tells us he supplied the information (III. 99), was an interesting pursuit, and for some time I was unable to get any information about it. Meantime an old map of the Prince's expedition belonging to Mr. George Lorimer, a member of this Society, was put into my hands, and another copy of the same map was found in the library of the Society of Antiquaries, Scot., but I could get no trace of its origin. The map has neither name, imprint, nor date. Its title runs thus:

'A General Map of Great Britain; Wherein are delineated the Mili-
'tary Operations in that Island during the years 1745 and 1746, and
'even the secret Routs of the Pr⸺⸺ after the Battle of Culloden until
'his Escape to France: Illustrated by An authentic Abstract of that
'interesting piece of History, and an exact chronological Table.'

On the left side a skeleton itinerary is engraved, and on the right side a series of paragraphs abstracting the principal events of the adventure. Throughout, the hero of the Enterprise is called the 'Pr⸺⸺'. The phraseology of the notes savoured of Bishop Forbes, and an error of the dates in South Uist,[1] and a change in the dates of Glenaladale's Narrative[2] made me think that this must be Finlayson's Map, but I could not be certain. I took it to the British Museum, but found no copy there. I had, however, the good fortune to meet Mr. Henry Jenner, himself a great-great-grand-nephew of John Finlayson, and I found that he, too, had been searching in vain for his kinsman's map. On seeing the chart I had brought and comparing it with a map of the Battle of Culloden in the Museum, already conjectured to be by Finlayson, the identity of style was at once apparent. But further evidence of authorship was forthcoming from manuscripts in the British Museum. John Finlayson is described in the list of the Culloden prisoners as engineer, and as belonging to the artillery (H.P.J. 611). In 1751[3] he was in custody for treason displayed in his Jacobite geographical work. In a petition to the Duke of Newcastle while in prison he asks for the restoration of his

---

[1] Cf. I. 268; *Itinerary*, p. 50, *n* I.
[2] III. 99; *Itinerary*, p. 57 *n*.
[3] The date of Bishop Forbes's reference to the Map is 18th Oct. 1751.

plates and maps,[1] which had been seized, and in this document he describes himself as a 'mathematical instrument maker at Edinburgh.'[2]

In a letter to Carlyll[3] he says :—

'Can there be treason in saying there was a Rebellion, and that the 'King's troops was twice worsted in Scotland? Can the bare recital of '·facts be injurious to the Government? Can saying the Pretender made 'an extraordinary escape from the diligent search made after him by the 'King's troops be deemed a panegyric? Can the saying that the Duke 'took advantage of his enemy's distress before the Battle of Culloden, 'and general-like forced them to battle, be any reflection?

'If the contraction Pr   give any offence it can be altered. At the same 'time it is evident the only reason of putting Pretender in that shape was 'but a harmless evivoque to make the map sell amongst a foolish set of 'people who thinks that word too harsh a term to express the person 'meant. I need not add that the facts are mostly collected from papers 'published by authority.'

In the notes engraved on the map,. Prince Charles Edward is more than thirty times alluded to as the 'Pr   ', and the reference to the Duke is, without any doubt, the following paragraph : 'And while great part 'of his army were dispersed in search of provisions, and others sunk down 'to rest through the fatigue of the double march, the Duke came upon 'them and forced the Battle of Culloden.'

The evidence thus adduced helped greatly to put the authorship of both maps beyond doubt.

The chart itself is of little geographical value. It shows England and Scotland and a portion of France. It is merely a skeleton outline with the counties and a few prominent places shown. The routes of the Prince and of the Government armies are shown in engraved lines tinted by hand, and the principal places mentioned in the Prince's wanderings are also figured ; but the rudimentary nature of the topography and the smallness of the scale make the map useless in locating their actual positions.

The scale approximates eighteen miles to the inch, and the size of the whole, which is printed on two sheets, is 39 inches high, by 26¾ inches broad, to outside of printed borders. The principal value of the map historically is the information engraved on the blank portions.

In the April number of the *Scottish Journal* of 1848, an itinerary of the Prince's movements is printed, which the editor believed to be an original document found in Aberdeen. It is in reality a copy of the notes on Finlayson's Map, probably made by some ardent Jacobite shortly after its publication.

---

[1] This shows there was more than one map, no doubt including the Culloden one.

[2] Add. MSS. British Museum, 28231, f. 97.

[3] *Ibid.* f. 93.

ADDITIONAL NOTE 9

THE PRINCE'S ESCAPE

IT has sometimes been suggested that the Government was not really anxious to capture Charles Edward ; but this idea may be dismissed on the direct authority of the Commander-in-chief, Lord Albemarle.

In a letter to the Duke of Newcastle announcing the Prince's escape, he says :—' Nothing is to me a more convincing proof of the disaffection of that part of the Country than that of His lying so long concealed amongst those people, and that he should be able to elude our narrowest and most exact searches, and at last make his escape notwithstanding the great reward offered to apprehend him ' (dated Edinburgh, Oct. 15, 1746, State Papers Domestic.   Cf. Captain Hay's remarks, I. 280).

POSTSCRIPT

LOCHGARRY'S NARRATIVE

AFTER the completion of this volume, the original manuscript of this brief soldier-like memorial or report from MacDonell of Lochgarry to his young chief was put at the disposal of the Society by Mr. Charles Fraser-Mackintosh, who had printed a short extract from it in his *Antiquarian Notes* on Inverness-shire (C.F.M. 257). The memorial is here printed in full, and forms a fitting ending to the narratives collected by Bishop Forbes.

From Lochgarry, we have some additional information about the negotiations at the beginning of the Enterprise; details of the number of clansmen engaged at different periods of the campaign; the reason for not following up the victory of Falkirk; the arrangements made for the Prince's safety in the later days of his wanderings; and here alone we have an indication of the route taken by the Prince in his journey from Lochaber to Badenoch, which has hitherto been only a matter of conjecture.

The manuscript consists of sixteen pages, small quarto paper, beautifully written, and, with the exception of the last leaf, is perfectly preserved. It is not dated, and there is nothing to show when it was written.

At the time that Lochgarry arrived in France, the old chief, John of Glengarry, and his eldest son Alexander (or Alastair), were both prisoners, the former in Edinburgh Castle, and the latter in the Tower.[1] From internal evidence, it may be assumed that the narrative was not composed immediately on reaching Paris, and it seems natural to believe that it was written for the information of young Glengarry after his release from the Tower, in the autumn of 1747.[2]

Although the character of the Highland chieftain to whom the Memorial is addressed has recently been seriously aspersed in *Pickle the Spy*, no suspicion of disloyalty has ever besmirched the fair fame of the

---

[1] See *Itinerary*, p. 5, *n.* 5.

[2] Young Glengarry's name, as Alexander MacDonald, captain in Lord John Drummond's regiment, is included in the list of prisoners captured in one of Drummond's transports by H.M.S. *Sheerness*, November 25th, 1745 (L.G. Nov. 26-29, *Itinerary*, p. 27, *n.* 3). In a letter to Cardinal York, June 1749, Glengarry states that he remained prisoner in the Tower for twenty-two months. (Stuart Papers, B.H. App. clxxxv.)

writer.   Lochgarry was one of those Highland gentlemen who, like
Cluny, had been gazetted to a commission in Lord Loudon's regiment,
in June 1745 (S.M. 298), but who joined Charles Edward at the beginning
of the Enterprise.   He was a member of the Prince's Council (*Itin.* p. 17,
n. 3), commanded the Glengarry clan during the march to Derby, while
Angus (or Æneas) MacDonell went back to the Highlands to collect reinforcements; and after the accidental death of that young chief at Falkirk,
he represented the great house of Glengarry to the end of the Enterprise.[1]

The manuscript is headed—

MEMORIAL, LOCHGARY TO GLENGARY

As to the Prince's landing, nobody is ignorant of.   He landed in
Arisaig in Clanronald's estate, he being the nearest Highland
chiftain to the coast : where immediately young Clanronald came
to His R[ll] H[s] and agreed to join the Roy[ll] standard, with all the
men he had on the mainland.   Immediatly his R. H[s]. sent him to
Sir Alexander and M'Leod to acquaint them of his landing safe,
and that his R. H[ness] expected they wou'd join his standard, which
it seems they declin'd, giving for reason that the Prince had no
force with him, and absolutely refused to join.   In the mean time
Glengarie's cousin-german Scotus waited of his R. H[s]. as one of
Glengary's near friends, and signified to the Prince that he was
sure that Glengary and his clan wou'd joine.   Some days after,
Glengary's brother, a young gentleman of about seventeen years
of age,[2] waited of his R. H[s]. and asured him, in his brother's
absence, that the whole family of Glengary wou'd join.   In the
mean time the Prince had sent M[c]Donell of Canlochmoydart to
the south of Scotland, whom he intrusted to acquaint Lochiel and
Keppoch that he was safe landed, and where they cou'd find him.
Upon which they both went immediatly to wait of his R. H[s].   They
both also agreed, after a short conference with him, to join his
standard.   Upon their return they had a meeting with Genr[l]
Gordon[3] and me.   I reason'd some time, and made some difficulty

---

[1] A good deal of information about Lochgarry's subsequent career is to be
found in *Pickle the Spy* ; in the Stuart Papers (B. H.), and in Mr. Mackenzie's
History of the MacDonalds (p. 343), where it is stated that in 1746 he was
between fifty and sixty years old.

[2] In Mr. Mackenzie's *History of the MacDonalds* (p. 349) Angus (or Æneas)
MacDonell is stated to have been nineteen years old, which seems more likely,
as he was a married man and the father of two children.

[3] John Gordon of Glenbucket, who was father-in-law of John of Glengarry.

to raise Glengarie's men, tho' at the same time your brother and I were ready to doe it, by the private instruction you had given before you left the country. Your brother at that time was gone at that time to the Laird of Strowan, intending to head his people, being married to his niece. Lochiel and Keppoch then told me, that in case Glengarie's men wou'd not join, they wou'd return to the Prince, and plainly tell him that their joining wou'd only expose his Roy^{ll} person with any men they cou'd make. By this I found they were positive not to join except I wou'd raise Glengarie's men. As I knew that the family of Glengarie were never defficient or absent when the Roy^{ll} family had the least to doe, and as I knew some time before your inclinations, made me immediatly declare what were your orders and my own intention before I came to this meeting, viz., that your people shou'd be ready to receive His Roy^{ll} H^s. at Laggan Achendroom, and conduct his Roy^{ll} person to the castle of Innergarie, your house. We certainly wou'd have all gone to his R. H^s. at the first setting up of his standard, but as he behoov'd to march thro' Glengary, it wou'd have proov'd unnecessary travel. Att our meeting here we found by information that there were three company's of George's forces to march from Inverness to Fort William, and other three of the same to march from Ruthven of Badenoch to escorte provisions to Fort Augustus. Upon this it was agreed that Keppoch shou'd attack the party going to Fort William, and I undertook to attack the party going to Fort Augustus, and had waited three days in ambush, with a part of Glengary's people, on the top of Corrierick; but, lucky for them, they came not, otherwise they had probably fared the same fates with them that were going to Fort William, who pass'd in two days thereafter, and within nine miles of Fort William, Keppoch attacked them personally, with his cousin Tiendrish, with about 50 men, and drove them backwards, on the king's road, being like an avenue, on the side of a steep hill, and a close wood, cou'd not attack them sword in hand. The enemy retreated about six miles till they came to the plain of Auchendroom, where fifty of the Glengary Kennedies turned out and join'd Keppoch, and after one smart fire attacked them sword in hand, upon which the enemy surrendered. This was the first sword drawn in the Prince's cause. The prisoners, officers and privat men, were sent under a strong guard to H^s. R. H^s. While I lay in ambush on Corrierick there passed one Capt Switnam, who commanded the barracks at Ruthven of Badenoch, and was going to Fort W[m]., as he was recon'd a very good ingeneer. I detatched four of the Glengary Kennedies to apprehend him, which they did effectually, horses, baggage, and servants.[1] I delivr'd him to Gen[l] Gordon, who delivred him to H. R. H[s].

Upon the 19th of Aug[t] the Roy[ll] standard was set up in Glenfinnan. On the 26th or 27th his R. H[s]., with Clanronald, Lochiel's and Keppoch's men, came to Laggan Auchentroom. Y[r] brother, who had met H. R. H[s]. at Ratlich, came up to me at Laggan, where I had all the Glengary men conveen'd. H. R. H[s]. arrived there at 8 o'clock at night, where I had the happiness to kiss his Roy[ll] H[s]. hand, and then marched with him to the Castle of Innergarie, and had the command of his guard that night. That same day young Scotus and young and old Barrisdales arrived at Auchendroom with your Cnoidart and Morar men, who made a very handsom appearance before the Prince, being compleatly armed, and most of them had targes.[2] The next day the Prince marched from Innergary to Aber Chalader, within six short miles of Corrierick. That night we had sure acc[tts] that Cope was come to Badenoch, and was coming next day for Corrierick, in order to attack the Prince and his army. Upon this H. R. H[s]. gave orders for an early rendezvous, in order to give him a[3] Cope on the top of Corrierick. We were all under arms about 7 o'clock in the morning, and marched towards the top of Corrierick. When we came to the top of the hill we gott sure accounts that Cope had been the night before at Ruthven o' Badenoch, and from thence had march'd strait to Innerness. Upon this acc[tt] we marched smartly to Garvalmore, where we came at 12 o'clock. The prince was positive at first to follow Cope, but upon H. R. H[s]. calling some of the princ[ll] people together, found it impracticable to overtake him before he reach'd Innerness. So it was determin'd to march directly south. H. R. H[s]. rested some days in Athol, and from thence march'd on to Perth, where Lord George Murray join'd us. We remaind some days there, and march'd from thence over the Forth, and came to Falkirk, where we encamped a night. Being informed that two regm[ts] of dragoons were at Linlithgow, we thought proper to attack them that night under the command of L[d] George, but they thought proper to retire, keeping in sight of us all next day. We then encamped twixt Lithgow and Edin[r]

---

[1] Stated in I. 352 to have been captured by Tiendrish (*Itin.* p. 7).

[2] Lochgarry gives his chief a detailed account of the gathering of the Clan. In the *Itinerary* the date is recorded (from L.P. and J.M.B.), when the whole clan had joined.   [3] *sic*, words apparently omitted.

The second night we came within two or three short miles of Edin[r], and twixt ten and eleven at night there was a detatchment of our reg[t], Keppoch's, Clanronald's, and Lochiel's, order'd to be ready to march into Edin[r]. I commanded yours; Glenaladel, Clanronalds; Lochiel, his; and, if I rightly remember, Tiendrish, Keppochs. We had a special good guide, and a very dark night. We marched very slowly, and managed our time so as to be at the port about break of day. Found the ports open, and enter'd without the stroak of a sword, and not the least opposition made in the town.

H. R. H[s]. and the rest of the army enter'd the town in the afternoon. We rested here three days, and having sure acc[tts] that Cope was landed at Dunbar, all necessary preparations were made to goe to meet him. Upon the 20th Sept[r] the Prince with his army marched from Dudiston to a height near Prestonpans, where we cou'd discern Cope and army drawn up in order o' battle in a very advantagious posture, with the sea in his rear, and a morass in his front and left flank. It was propos'd for a long time to fight him that night, but at last agreed to rest on our arms all night, and attack him by break o' day; which was accordingly done, and had the desired effect.

About two hours before daylight we were all drawn up without the least noise. We immediatly march'd on, very quiet, and without the least noise, and came directly in a line o' battle about break o' day. All engaged on our side were as follows :—

Of your men,	.	.	.	.	500 [1]
Clanronalds,	.	.	.	.	300
Keppochs,	.	.	.	.	300
Glenco's,	.	.	.	.	120
Camerons,	.	.	.	.	500
Stuarts,	.	.	.	.	200
			Totall,		1900 [sic]

There was likewise engaged a few M[c]Grigors, I can't condescend on the number. This was our first line, and only engaged, and gain'd as compleat a victory as ever was gain'd, having made prisoners of all who were not kill'd, excepting a few horse, who made their escape w[t]. Genr[l] Cope. You see of the number

---

[1] Cf. Appendix, p. 91. The Grants of Glenmoriston are here included in the Glengarry regiment.

engag'd there were 1200 M⁰Donnells.   After the fight the Prince
and army went into Ed^r, with all their prisoners, baggage, etc.
Some days thereafter the Prince call'd a council of war, wherein
it was determin'd that a gentleman from each chief shou'd goe
home, to bring out what men remain'd there.   Your brother went
home to bring out yours, and in order Strowan's people shou'd be
brŏt out.

About the beginning o' Novr the Prince call'd a council o'
war, wherein H. R. H^s. determin'd to march into England with
the forces he then had, and not to wait those who were coming
up, but order'd them to follow.

We march'd on without halt till we came to Brampton, near
Carlile, where the Prince rested with part o' the army, and order'd
the siege of Carlile, which surrender'd after four days siege.   The
next day after the surrender, the Prince enter'd the town with his
whole army, where H.R.H^s. remain'd some days.   From thence he
march'd straight with his whole army till he arrived at Darby,
where he rested two days; and H.R.H^s. called a council o' war,
and finding most of the private people of the army's opinion to be
rather to retreat than goe forward (tho' at the same time H.R.Hs.'
opinion and inclination was to goe forward), he agreed to a
retreat.   Consequently, we began our retreat next day.   Lord
George Murray, who always had the rear, chose our regm^t for the
rearguard, tho' it was not our turn.   When we came to Kendal,
we had acc^{tts} of the enemy's being close in our rear; and our regm^t
having the rearguard, and likewise the charge of the artillery.   The
Prince marched on with the army till they arrived at Penrith, and
the weather very terrible, the rear cou'd not reach Chap that
night, which is halfway twixt Penrith and Kendal.   Ld George
took up our quarters in a little villiage, where we rested that night
on our arms, without thro'ing a stitch of cloaths, as we were sure
the enemy was very near us.   Next day we marched by daylight,
and for want of proper horses the artillery was very fashious, and
a last load with cannon shot happening to break on the road, upon
Lord George's giving a hearty dram to the men, they carried,
some one, some two, some three of the shot, with all their arms
and acuterments.   All this day some of the enemy's horse were
in our rear, but made no attack.   This night we came to Chap,
and after placing our guards and sentinelles, Lord George, the
other gentlemen, and I, took up our quarters about 8 o'clock at
night.   Some of the enemy's horse had come up and attacked our

guards, which occasion'd our being the second night under arms, without any kind of rest.   By this time the Prince and army had got ten miles before us, and lay that night at Penrith.   By the break o' day Ld George order'd to beat to arms, and order'd the artillery on before.   We marched on, expecting every minut the enemy wou'd be up with us, having none with us but your regm^t and about one hundred and twenty of Roy Stuart's regm^t.   About halfway to Penrith, we saw at some distance, to the number of about 5 or 600 horse, whom we took to be part of our own army; but upon coming near us they made a form to attack us.   These were militia sent to interrupt our march ; but by a detatchment we sent to attack them giving them a smart fire, which kill'd two or three of them, they were routed, and fled, so we march'd on untill we came to Clifton, within two short miles of Penrith, where the Prince and his army lay.   Here Ld George gott account that some of the enemy were come to the house of Lowtherhall, about a mile's distance on our left.   He desired me to ask the men (as he knew they were fatigued) if they were willing to attack that house.   They answer'd me that they were most willing.   Upon which we marched and surrounded the house, and only found in it one officer, with a footman of the Duke of Cumberland's, whom he had sent before to take up quarters for him.   Upon our return to Clifton, we perceived the enemy to the number of about 3000 horse, advanced by this time within $^1/_4$ of a mile of Clifton.   Cluny and his McPhersons, to about the number of three hundred men, happened to be at this village.   Ld George ordered them on one post on the side of the road, and our regm^t on another on the other side.   It was then about nightset, when the enemy, being all horse, dismounted—I can't condescend on their number, being then dark—and attack'd the McPhersons, who received them, and after a close fire for some time on both sides, the enemy were repulsed.   Upon this they sent a stronger body to attack us both, which came directly up to us, and it being then quite dark, they coming very close to us, we only heard the noise of their boots, and could plainly discern their yellow belts.   We first received their full fire, which did us little damage.   We immediatly gave them ours, and then attacked them sword in hand, and oblidged them to retreat with a considerable loss.

Ld. George them marched with us and the McPhersons into the town, where we found the whole army ready to march for Carlisle, so that we had neither time to refresh ourselves, or men.   So you

may judge our condition, having marched t[w]o days without resting from Kendal to Penrith, which is long 20 miles, and, without
halt, 16 more on to Carlisle, all without any sleep and very little
provision; yet we brōt all the artillery safe, and lost very few men
at the attack at Clifton.   I rec^d a small wound there myself in
the knee, and no other gentleman touched.   We stay'd two
nights at Carlisle.   The third day in the morning by break o'
day we marched, expecting surely to meet Cumberland that day
to give him battle; but, perceiving no enemy, march'd forward,
and that night crossed the Esk.   H.R.H^s. continued on his march
without any remarkable occurencies till he arrived safe with his
army at Glasgow.   The Prince stay'd some days at Glasgow to
refresh his army, and then marched to Bannokburn, near Stirling.
There we remained till our army from the north came up and
join'd us.   Your brother join'd us here with a strong reinforcement to your regm^t; we then made two batallions, your people
of Urquhart and Glenmorison having likewise join'd us.   We
muster'd then directly twixt nine hundred and a thousand men,
which being devided, your brother commanded the first and I the
second batallion.   Barrisdale likewise join'd us on the battle-day
with 300 clever fellows from the north, which made us compleat
1200 on the day of battle.   Some days after this, Genr^l Hally
arrived with his army at Falkirk, where he encamped.   Our army
was three different days drawn up, expecting they wou'd give us
battle; but the enemy still keeping their ground, a rendezvous
was ordered of our whole army on the 17th Janry, where a
general council o' war was called by H.R.H^s., wherein it was
determin'd to march and attack the enemy.   Consequently we
marched, and came upon the hill above Falkirk where they were
encamped, and drew up in order of battle.   By this time Genr^{ll}
Hally had his army likewise drawn up in order of battle.   Having
his whole horse on his front, he sent them immediatly to attack
our right, where the whole McDonells were posted as they were
at Gladsmuir.   No man cou'd attack more bravely or with more
resolution that the enemy did.   They came within 7 or 8 yards of
our men, who received their fire before they burnt a priming;
their fire doing us little damage, we gave them our fire, which put
them in the utmost confusion and totall deroute; what were alive
of them made the best of their way off the field.   They were
likewise attacked on the left, but can't inform you of the
particulars that happen'd there.   By this time there was a

generall halt call'd thro' the army, by whose orders I never can learn hitherto. The weather by this time was most tempestous, and growing late and dark. Our men during the halt were quite stiffned, after the former heat and furry they were in time of action; and finding the enemy had left the field and retreated towards Edinburgh, and many of them never halted till they were at Musselburg, and severall miles beyond it, which is at least 24 miles from the field of battle.

The Prince, Ld George, and severall gentlemen of the army, went into Falkirk about 7 o'clock at night. All the enemy's artillery and most of their baggage were taken. We were all in top spirits, and, I beleve, had certainly followed Mr Hally, had not the melancholy and misfortunate accident of your brother's death happen'd,[1] who was ador'd and regretted by H.R.H^s. and the whole army. His death really dispirited the whole Highlanders very much. He was three days alive after his wound. During this time there was a generall desertion in the whole army. The Prince then went to his former quarters at Bannokburn; and being inform'd that great numbers of our men had gone home, resolved to march north, which he began to doe next day, and continued his march with his army till he arrived at Moyhall, M'Intosh house. H.R.H^s. was there inform'd that Lord Loudon and the president were at Innerness with about 2000; but upon his R.H^s.' approach, they thought proper to retire immediatly in a hurry, and crossed the ferry of Keisig, near Innerness, and secured all the boats on his own side the water, so that he cou'd not be followed, unless we had gone round an arm of the sea, at least 20 miles in circuit. There he was immediatly followed by a detatchment of the Prince's army commanded by Lord Cromarty. Loudon and army marched still forward and crossed the great ferry, till he arrived at Dornok. Here Loudon secur'd likewise all the boats, and carried them to his side the water, so that there was no possibility of reaching him, as the circuit of the ferry wou'd be about sixty miles, and the whole country where he lay were disafected to the Roy^{ll} cause, being Sutherland's lands.

As Loudon lay secure in this place, the Prince had ordered our regm^t, Clanronald's, Stuart's of Appin, Frazer's and McGrigor's, to join Cromarty, who had then the command. We all join'd at

---

[1] Accidentally shot by one of Clanranald's clansmen in the streets of Falkirk (L.P. 503).

Dingwall, and march'd from that to the town of Tayne, upon the south side of the Ferry, opposite to Lord Loudon's headquarters. Here we stay'd for some time, and cou'd not gett a boat tho we had given a thousand guineas for one. In this situation we lay sometimes, and in the interior, H.R.H^s. found a proper person to bring us boats sufficient to transport us at once to the other side of the water, where Loudon lay. The boats being at last arrived undiscovered by the enemy, occasioned by a very thick mist that one man cou'd not discern another at ten paces distance. As the boats arrived only at 10 o'clock at night, and not being in time acquainted of their arrival, the tide left them dry on the beech, about half a mile from the sea. We gott all to arms in order to launch them; but as they were heavy boats, it took us a long time before we cou'd sett them afloat. So by the time we gott them ready the enemy cou'd fairly discern us; but we resolved at any rate to make the attempt, which seem'd very dangerous had our enemys made a right use of it, especially as we were little more than half their number, they being two thousand, including Loudon's own regm^t, and our number was as follows: Our regm^t, 530; Clanronalds, 300; Stuarts, 200; Frazers, 300; McGrigors, 100 men. Upon our landing (to our great surprize) we found no opposition; Loudon and the president were quarter'd very near the place where we landed, and had discovered us in time eneough to make their escape. We were at this time command'd by James Duke o' Perth. At our landing, and seeing no enemy, it was determin'd strait to Dornoch about 6 miles distance, which was Loudon's headquarters, and where we certainly expected to meet him upon our approach to that place. The laird of McIntosh, cap^t in Loudon's regm^t, and Major McKenzie of the same, with sevr^l other officers, came and surrendred themselves prisioners, with all the men under their command, among which were a good number of Loudon's own regiment. Capt Stack of Laly's regm^t and I received the arms of the whole prisioners.

Next day we pursued Loudon and the president, but cou'd not come up with them, as it always happens them that are running to save their lives outmarch their pursuers. We remain'd some time in this country, untill we were called to Innerness, some days before the battle o' Culloden, which I shant offer to give a detail of, as I'm sure you can have a great many different acc^{tts} of it from severall gentlemen about you.

The McDonells had the left that day, the Prince having agreed

to give the right to Ld George and his Atholmen.   Upon which
Clanronald, Keppoch, and I spoke to his R.H^s. upon that subject,
and begg'd he wou'd allow us our former right, but he intreated
us for his sake we wou'd not dispute it, as he had already agreed
to give it to Lord George and his Atholmen ; and I heard H.R.H^s.
say that he ressented it much, and shou'd never doe the like if he
had occasion for it.   Your Reg^t that I had the hon^r to command
at this battle was about 500 strong, and that same day your
people of Glenmorrison were on their way to join us, and likewise
about 100 Glengary men were on their march to join us, on the
other side of Lochness.   Att this unlucky battle [we] were all on
the left, and near us on our right were the brave McLeans,[1] who
wou'd have been about 200, as well looked men as ever I saw com-
manded by McLean of Drumnine,[2] one of the princi^{ll} gentlemen of
that clan ; he and his son were both kill'd on the spot, and I belive
50 of their number did not come of the field.   Their leader
waited of the Prince on his landing, with a comission from most
of the princ^{ll} gentlemen of that clan, who were always known
to be among the first in the field, when the Roy^{ll} family had to
doe, and wou'd have been all in arms at this time, had not been
the unlucky accident of their chiefs being in the Government's
hand, which was a genr^{ll} loss to the cause, and occasion'd that
this brave clan were not all in the field ; they live likewise under
the jurisdiction of the Duke of Argile, since the forfeiture of this
great estate, occasiond by thir constant early attatchment to the
Roy^{ll} family, so consequently live in the neighbourhood of the
numerous clan of the Campbells, who were always dissafected to
the Roy^{ll} cause, and if they had all risen in arms their familys
woud have been quite ruin'd by them, but if their chief had
had been at their head, this they wou'd have little regarded.
However I'm sure, including the 200 at Culloden, with severall and those
other young gentlemen that had join'd, the severall regm^{ts} of the Lochiel had
McDonells woud have compleated twixt four and five hundred and other
men of that clan. parts.

out of Morven

H.R.H^s. being close to our line in time of the action, and seeing
at last such a totall deroute of his army was obliged to retire.
The horse he rode himself was shot under him, and one of his
servants killed by his side with a cannon ball ; he happend to
have none of the leading people then about him, or any who

---

[1] This does not quite corroborate Finlayson's map (*ante*, p. 97).

[2] Cf. *Itinerary*, p. 22, *n.* 3.

knew the country well, and as there was no rendezvous ordered,[1]
as we expected to beat the enemy, as we had always done before,
and which we had certainly done at this time had it not been
our being overnumber'd, and great fatigue we were in, and severall
disadvantages too tedious to relate, as you'll learn these particulars from severalls about you.   I have heard his R. Hˢ. often
regrett that a place of rendezvous had not been ordered, which
occasioned that the princˡˡ people who escaped from the battle
not meeting with H.R.Hˢ., and as he had none with him who
knew the country, he was oblidg'd to retire to the west coast,
and from thence took an open boat to the Isle of Ouist belonging to Clanronald, where H.R.Hˢ. stay'd lurking till June, when
the enemy got information of his being there, upon which they
poured in troops to the country, both regular and militia, and
besides had surrounded the isle with men o' war, so that there
was no possibility apparently of his R. Hˢ. making his escape.
But by the means of Hugh MᶜDonell, of Sir Alexʳˢ family, who
contrived to send the lucky Flora MᶜDonell to conduct his Royˡˡ Hˢ.
in womens dress, by which he escaped ; but as the whole isles were
swarming with the enemy he cou'd not be there safe two nights
in one place.   From thence he landed in the Isle of Sky on Sir
Alexʳˢ ground, and by the means of another gentleman (MᶜDonald
of Kingsburg), a friend and relation of Sir Alexander's, also made
his escape from that country till he landed on the mainland at a
place called Malaik, in Glengaries estate, in July.   By this time all
Cumberland's army was alarmed of his R.Hˢ. being chased from
the Isles, and of his landing on the main ; upon which the most of
their army was detatched, and a line made of them near the coast,
and parties put on every pass, so that it appear'd impossible that
he coud gett thro' them undiscovered.   At this time H.R.Hˢ. had
sent for, or accidentaly met, with MᶜDonell of Glenaladel, and
two or three more, and luckily made their escape thro' the guards
in the night-time.   They travell'd two or three days thro' the hills,
till at last Glenaladel lost knowledge of the ground, and knew not
where he was going.   They were then on the hills which march
'twixt Glengary and Seaforth, where accidentally and luckily they
met four of the Glengary MᶜDonells,[2] who had been oblig'd to

---

[1] Cf. *Itin.* p. 45 *n.*

[2] Of the eight Glenmoriston men, three were Chisholms and one a MacGregor
(III. 202).   The other four (two MacDonells, a Grant, and a MacMillan) had no
doubt belonged to the Glengarry regiment, and are alone noticed by Lochgarry.

shun the enemy to take to the hills, with their wives, children, and cattle. They, notwithstanding of their Prince's disguise, knew him, tho' he appeared quite a different person from what they had seen him at the head of his army, and with tears in their eyes they fell on their knees and thanked God that his Roy[ll] person was safe. They knew also Glenaladel, who told them he had lost his way, and did not know where to goe, and asked them which was the safest route for H.R.H[s]. They immediatly said they woud abandon their wives and everything that was dear to them; as they knew the hills they woud doe what was in their power to find out for his R.H[s]. a safe lurking place, and bring his R.H[s]. what provision the country can afford. Upon which they conducted his R.H[s]. to a cove in one of the greatest hills in Scotland, within 15 or 16 miles of Cumberland's camp at Fort Augustus. One of these four men went day about for intelligence and other necessarys for his R.H[s].; and so secret and cautious they were in their office that they never went near their wives and familys from the minute they met their Prince, and their poor wives concluded they were either kill'd, or taken by the enemy. They knew well the reward declar'd to give for apprehending or destroying H.R.H[s]., but all the bribes in the world cou'd not make them betray that trust. I believe no other nation in the world can produce common fellows wou'd doe the like. H.R.H[s]. enquired if they cou'd find me out to him; at this time the enemy lay twixt me and them, and rendred it impossible for me to cross over the waters who were prodigious high by the great falls of rain about that time. There were three different attacks made on me, as the enemy knew where I skulked; I faced them fairly every time and beat them off, by which they lost severalls killd and wounded, this was but a small affair, but the only blood drawn from the enemy after the Battle o' Culloden.

The Prince had stay'd twixt twenty days and a month in this cave.[1] By this time your four men that were with him gott intelligence of me, and where I skulk'd, upon which his R. H[s]. came directly near that place, and sent on of them for me. This was on Aug[t]., I can't remember the day of the month.[2] I came directly where his Roy[ll] H[s]. was, and was overjoyed to kiss his hand. It gave me new courage to see his R. H[s]. safe, and really believed, once I had the happiness to meet H.R.H[s]., he woud be afterwards safe in spite of his enemys. This night we had no kind of pro-

---

[1] See *ante*, p. viii, *n.* I.   [2] August 15th.

vision but a wild deer one of our men killd just near the hut. Next day Glenaladel kiss'd H.R.H[s]. hand, took leave, and went home to his own house near the west coast, his H[s]. intrusting to him that in case there came any ships from France, he shou'd acquaint him, and gave him a trace to find him, in case that happened.

After he left us we changed our lodgings and made up a new castle, where we made shift for some time for provisions, and had always intelligence from the enemy, as we lay within 14 miles of their encampment. I being one evening out walking with H.R.H[s]., I took the liberty to ask his R.H[s]. what he intended to doe ; upon which I told him that there was still a considerable party wou'd rise in arms (tho at this time the Master of Lovat[1] had delivred himself up to the enemy), and I believed he wou'd very soon make a flying army of about two thousand men, and that the people were so terribly exasperated against Cumberland for his cruel behaviour that one of them wou'd be worth two before the battle, and wou'd be much the safest way for his R.H[s]. person, and as there was now plenty of money, his army wou'd turn soon very numerous, especially as the affection generally of the whole kingdom was now for him. As his R.H[s]. agreed that these proposals were right, he proposed to send to Lochiel and Cluny. I engaged Glengarie's people shou'd be all ready in eight and forty hours, and obliged myself that with them I shoud attack and surprize Fort Augustus, and destroy or apprehend all the enemy there, being at that time about 800 men twixt regular and militia. Upon this the Prince proposed to send for Cap[t]. Arch. Cameron, Lochiel's brother, as I did not know where Lochiel and Cluny skulk'd. Jn[o]. Murray some time before had gone of and left the money with Lochiel. We waited then for Arch. Cameron, his R.H[s]. intending to send him and me with the message to Lochiel and Cluny. During this time I kept out about twenty Kennedies, who, I was sure, wou'd keep us from being surpriz'd. Some days thereafter Arch. Cameron arrived.[2] Next day the Prince sent him and me to Lochiel and Cluny to see if they wou'd come into the proposals, and once there was any body of men together, H.R.H[s]. wou'd send a proper person to the Court of France, or goe himself, if all we his loyall subjects thought it more proper. Upon this Mr. Cameron and I kiss'd his R.H[s]. hand, and parted to execute our comission. After 5 or 6 days and nights travelling thro' the hills in order to shun our enemy's, we arrived at the place where

---

[1] Simon Fraser's submission to Loudon is dated August 10th. [2] August 20th.

Lochiel and Cluny stay'd.   We told them our comission from To whose
H.R.H[s].   They answered, in their opinion, as the kingdom was so care was he in-
full of the enemy, it wou'd be of much worse consequence to rise you and
in arms than doe otherwise.   Upon which we immediatly returnd Doctor
to our Prince[1] and told him our answer; upon which his R.H[s]. came Cameron were
to a resolution (tho, I dare say, much against his inclination, and absent?[2]
he wou'd have rather been at the head of an army, as he propos'd)
to join Lochiel and Cluny, in order to consult the most expedient
way of going over to France.

Next day we prepared ourselves in order to travel day and night
till we shou'd arrive at Lochiel and Cluny.   I then gott together my
trusty and brave party of fifty men, of your people, devinding them
in two's and three's, and sent them to different arts[3] for fear of being
surpriz'd on our march by the enemy, they being spread over the
whole country.   We were oblidg'd to pass within two short miles of
Fort Augustus,[4] where the body of the enemy lay encamped, but were
in no danger of a surprize, by the vigilance of our little detatchment.

We travell'd in this manner three days and nights without much
eating or any sleep, but slumbering now and then on a hillside.[5]   Our
indefatigable Prince bore this with greater courage and resolution
than any of us, nor never was there a Highlander born cou'd travel
up and down hills better or suffer more fatigue.   Show me a king or
prince in Europe cou'd have born the like, or the tenth part of it.

H.R.H[s]. arrived at last where Lochiel and Cluny were.   We
remain'd there four nights,[6] and the 5th we received account from
Glenaladel that there were two frigats arrived at Arrisaig in Loch-
nanouah.   We all set of next day very early, having about one
hundred miles to travell to where the ships were.   We embark'd
the 29th Sept[r].,[7] and arrived at Paris the 14th 8[ber].

---

[1] They were absent from the 21st to 27th August.

[2] This question is written on the back of the manuscript, presumably by
Young Glengarry.   The Prince's companions seem then to have been Rev. John
Cameron, Cameron of Clunes, Captain MacRaw ; and probably Glenaladale and
Patrick Grant were in the neighbourhood (I. 99 ; *Itinerary*, p. 66, *n*. 1).

[3] Generally written ' airts '=different directions.

[4] This is the only information I have been able to discover about the Prince's
route to Badenoch.

[5] The party, according to Cluny and John Cameron, left Torvault on August
28th, met Lochiel at Mellaneuir on the 30th, where Cluny joined them on
September 1st (*Itinerary*, p. 68).

[6] Eight nights according to Cluny (*Ibid.* p. 70).

[7] A New Style date (Lochgarry was writing in France), but it should be Sept.
30th.   According to Cluny, corroborated by Hugh Macdonald (III. 46, 52), and in-
directly by the Prince (*Itin.*, p. 70, *n*. 4), the party went on board Sept. 19th, O.S.

The number of the clans engaged in the first line which only engaged that day was as follows, viz. at Falkirk—

Glengary, ...	1200 men
Keppoch, ...	500 do.
Clanronald, ...	350
Glenco, ...	120
McDonells, .	2170
Lochiel, ...	900
McPhersons, ...	300
Stuarts, ...	300
McIntoshes, ...	400
Frasers, ...	400
Farqrsons, ...	150
Other clans, .	2450

Now, you may observe what number McDonells were at each battle; and I dare say without any selfishness, that none of the battles cou'd have been won without them; and further, I say that these and their followers, under God, had the good fortune to save his Royll Hs. person. I hear there are severalls giving in Memorials of the Prince's expedition that never saw a priming burnt in the Cause, tho' they can only give them by hearsay at the fireside. For my part, I was eye and ear witness to all I have here related. I'm not very positive as to the other [clans'] numbers at the battle o' Falkirk except the McDonells, but [I am] sure their numbers were near the above calculation.

As to Mr. Ker's writting on this subject, he must be but , ... ignorant concerning our clans, so I can't see what he can [say on] that head; all I know about him is that he is very brave, was aid de camp to Ld George, and if the whole aid de camps [had] minded their duty on the day o' Falkirk, the affair wou'd have [been] otherwise, for I can attest there was none of them seen from [right to] left during the whole time o' the action.

D. McDONELL of LOCHGARY.

INDEX

THE END